Journey to Men

25 Awesome Missions

to

Teach Boys Resourcefulness

Paul Van Lierop

JTM Publishing
Bozeman, Montana
2019

First paperback edition May 2019

Book Cover Design by Damonza
Original Illustrations by Yilmaz Dagli
Additional Illustrations from the War Department FM

ISBN 978-1-7339777-0-8 (paperback)
ISBN 978-1-7339777-1-5 (ebook)

journeytomen.com

Paul Van Lierop
P.O. Box 11152
Bozeman, MT 59719

For Tim and Silas,

I wrote these missions for you, but when I began I did not understand that one of you would reach manhood before they were published. Perhaps one day your kids will complete these same missions with you. I'm beyond proud to be called your dad.

Contents

PARENT GUIDE 3
WHY THIS BOOK? 3
WHO'S THIS BOOK FOR? 4
IS THIS BOOK FOR BOYS ONLY? 4
MOTIVATING YOUR KIDS 5
INTRODUCTION TO THE MISSIONS 7

COMPONENTS OF A MISSION 7
THE CONCEPT OF MAN POINTS 8
INDIVIDUAL MISSION COMPONENTS 8
THE COMPONENTS OF THE CELEBRATION 13
LOCATION FOR THE CELEBRATION 13
CEREMONIAL GIFTS FOR BOYS 13

THE CELEBRATION OF MAN 13
CELEBRATION OF MAN ACTIVITIES 14
THE ACTUAL CELEBRATION OF MAN 14
AFTER ACTION REPORT 15
PRINTABLE MISSION GUIDES 17

MISSION OVERVIEW 17
MISSION 1: OPERATION TIMBUKTU 18
MISSION 2. OPERATION METAKNIFE 20
MISSION 3: OPERATION GOOD NEIGHBOR 22
MISSION 4: OPERATION INFERNO 24
MISSION 5: OPERATION PACKMULE 26
MISSION 6: OPERATION PENNYPINCH 28
MISSION 7: OPERATION RISE AND SHINE 30
MISSION 8: OPERATION BROKENSPOKE 32

MISSION 9: OPERATION GAS PUMPER 34

MISSION 10: OPERATION KICKSTART 35

MISSION 11: OPERATION CONDOR 37

MISSION 12: OPERATION CLEAN SWEEP 39

MISSION 13: OPERATION KNOT MY JOB 40

MISSION 14: OPERATION AVOCATION 41

MISSION 15: OPERATION PERSEVERANCE 43

MISSION 16: OPERATION WHEELS ON THE BUS 45

MISSION 17: THE MACGYVER CHALLENGE 46

MISSION 18: OPERATION FALLING WATER 48

MISSION 19: OPERATION CORRESPONDENCE 50

MISSION 20: OPERATION FOXHOLE 52

MISSION 21: OPERATION TIME CRISIS 54

MISSION 22: OPERATION SAFEHOUSE 56

MISSION 23: OPERATION BLOWOUT 57

MISSION 24: OPERATION BUGOUT 59

MISSION 25: OPERATION SKIDMARK 61

MISSION POINT TALLY **63**

SUGGESTED MAN POINT TARGETS 65

FEEDBACK REQUESTED **67**

BOOK REVIEW 67

MISSION PICTURES AND FEEDBACK 67

CADET GUIDE (KIDS ONLY) **68**

Missions

KNIFE GUIDE 74

OPERATION TIMBUKTU 77

OPERATION METAKNIFE 81

OPERATION GOOD NEIGHBOR 85

OPERATION INFERNO 89

OPERATION PACKMULE 95

OPERATION PENNYPINCH 101

OPERATION RISE AND SHINE 107

OPERATION BROKENSPOKE 113

OPERATION GAS PUMPER 119

OPERATION KICKSTART 125

OPERATION CONDOR 131

OPERATION CLEANSWEEP 137

OPERATION KNOT MY JOB 143

OPERATION AVOCATION 149

OPERATION PERSEVERANCE 155

OPERATION WHEELS ON THE BUS 159

THE MACGYVER CHALLENGE 165

OPERATION FALLING WATER 169

OPERATION CORRESPONDENCE 175

OPERATION FOXHOLE 181

OPERATION TIME CRISIS 187

OPERATION SAFEHOUSE 193

OPERATION BLOWOUT 199

OPERATION BUGOUT 205

OPERATION SKIDMARK 211

PARENT
GUIDE

CHAPTER 1

///

PARENT GUIDE

Why This Book?

The idea for this book came from an afternoon drive listening to one of my favorite podcasts. In the story, the narrator had discovered that he had cancer with only 6 months to live. The story continued with the narrator describing everything he planned to do with his remaining time and the things that suddenly mattered little. I found myself very emotional by the end of the podcast and I knew why. I realized that if I was to die tomorrow, I would have left my two boys without fundamental skills I'd intended to pass on. Skills that would help them on their journey to being capable men and productive resourceful members of society. How could I possibly be so busy that I neglected to pass on those important life lessons? Further I didn't see a timeline where this would naturally happen.

My wife and I brainstormed mission ideas on a long road trip which would ultimately turn into "Missions to Manhood." These missions would be standalone lessons to teach independence and resourcefulness. I witnessed repeatedly my two boys "watching" rather than experiencing the world around them. Technology is causing the world to become smaller while our kid's experiences and curiosity have narrowed as well. As a boy, if I wanted to learn a hobby or how to build a fort I had three options. 1. I could experiment on my own using trial and error. 2. I could somehow get myself to the library and locate a resource to teach me about the topic. 3. I could find a local expert on the subject and ask them for help.

My kid's first inclination is to turn to YouTube or a search engine to fill a knowledge gap. While it is amazing the breadth of information available with a few taps what gets lost is the drive for exploration and resourcefulness. Create a scenario for the kids where they have a lack of resources but a goal they need to accomplish and a reward for doing that and watch what happens. That's the basis for our Missions to Manhood and I have seen firsthand the change in my own boys thinking and behavior. Wouldn't it be great to have kids that would take initiative, explore, make mistakes instead of waiting around for someone else to figure things out for them in a 10 minute online video? Just the people we need raising the next generation, solving the worlds problems and giving back.

Who's This Book For?

The missions to manhood were originally written for the Author's two boys at the age of 11 and 13. There is latitude in many of the missions for a wide range of participant ages. It's simple enough to tweak some mission parameters to cater to younger children. During the initial mission rollout participants ranged from 6 to 16 and all took something away from the missions. The ideal age target would be between 9-14.

Is This Book for Boys Only?

Absolutely not. The language and tone of the missions is written specifically to boys but by no means should that prevent girls from taking part. Most of the missions would be relevant and interesting for boys and girls alike.

Motivating Your Kids

It is extraordinarily difficult as a parent to let your kids fail. We have terms like helicopter parent or even snow plow parent for those parents who will do everything in their power to knock down their children's boundaries. One of the greatest gifts we can give our children is the freedom to learn, experience and yes fail on their own. The missions in Journey to Men are designed to be fun while challenging.

You are free to choose any mission order but it's highly recommended that you choose a task that won't be misconstrued as work or chores. This is not Operation Clean Sweep or Operation Skidmark. Operation Timbuktu which is the first of our missions provides a backdrop for your child to find some freedom and catch the vision for Journey to Men. What we've seen through a full summer of mission trials both with the author's kids and a host of other families is that once they can navigate you to a destination of their choosing, they are in.

If you're noticing a lack of motivation even after the first mission perhaps sit down and explain the mechanics of the Journey to Men which leads to the Celebration of Man. One parent used the Man Point system to provide a series of prizes at multiple phases as it motivated their kids to keep going like a snowball effect.

CHAPTER 2

///

Components of a Mission

Introduction to the Missions

We developed Journey to Men as an entertaining way to
encourage kids to be more resourceful, independent and
responsible. These aren't assignments, they are missions.
You aren't their Mom or Dad you are their Commanding
Officer (C.O.). The missions are standalone activities
that provide just enough information and reference all
the relevant resources to complete. Give your children
permission to succeed or fail on their own merit. They'll
have fun doing it and feel a real sense of pride and
accomplishment at the conclusion. Do everything in your
power to avoid intervening or help them with their missions
unless called for in the briefing. In doing so, you'll help instill
a spirit of independence and resourcefulness, skills that will
serve them well in their adult lives.

Missions vary in their focus, locale and time duration. For
instance, Operation Penny Pinch involves saving up money
over time and may not require a lot of time on the day
you assign the mission. Other missions like the MacGyver
Challenge might take them the whole day to complete.
Some missions are outdoors while some are more indoor
related. The benefit is that you can choose which mission is
appropriate for the timeframe, location and level of busyness

in your squad. Most missions work just as well on vacation as they do at headquarters. By all means include friends, family and neighbors in the activities.

The Concept of Man Points

Each mission that your child completes will equate to an amount of "man points." There are a variety of ways to earn bonus man points, and also ways to lose man points (leaving a messy work area). At the end of a series of missions if they have earned enough man points they can attend the "Celebration of Man." We'll talk more about the Celebration of Man later, they will not want to miss it. Provided in Chapter 5 is a mission checklist that gives total points per mission and suggested totals for qualification. These are guidelines only, it's up to your judgement to figure out their required points based on your own children's motivations. One of our boys got stressed out about his point totals as the missions went on, so we took a more liberal approach with him. His brother was intent on getting the exact amount of points necessary and that was a perfect motivator for him.

It's a mechanism that rewards your child for doing the things you appreciate and value. Behaving in a manner inappropriate for a Journey to Men cadet can also cost man points. Just don't add or subtract the points arbitrarily, be sure they know why they got or lost man points.

Individual Mission Components

All missions include similar components so that your cadet can quickly understand the key information needed to start their mission. If your cadet has the tendency to skip the details encourage them to keep the mission guide with them to be sure they hit all the key requirements and earn the maximum man points.

Mission Brief

Here you'll find a high-level overview of the mission at hand that may also include a bit of a backstory. Perhaps you are saving your village from an Egyptian gas ant invasion or saving the town from a roving biker gang.

Equipment

In most cases we will include a comprehensive list of resources required to complete the mission. To make preparation for the missions easier on the C.O.'s the mission guide details the resources necessary. You can also go to the website https://journeytomen.com/resources/ for direct links to purchase the more difficult to find items. A primary goal of Journey to Men is resourcefulness and some missions will require the cadet to gather material available locally, whether it be tree branches, shelter materials or other miscellaneous items.

Mission Details

Each mission is designed to be standalone and for the most part can be done in any particular order. The mission guide provides enough information to complete the particular mission steps but by no means are we discouraging the cadet for researching or looking for additional information. In fact several missions require them to do just that in order to complete the mission. In all things related to Journey to Men we encourage the participant to figure things out for themselves as much as possible.

Mission Points

At the end of the mission guide will be a rundown of possible mission points AKA "Man Points." This is not meant to be a disciplinary tool or a way to find fault with their completion of the mission rather it's a way to reward them for a job well done, for following the directions and completing the mission. Some missions include point deductions for such reasons as an untidy workspace. If your cadet is stressed out about getting enough points, ease off on the overall tallying, that's not the point of the missions.

CHAPTER 3

The Celebration of Man

The "Celebration of Man" culminates the 25 Missions to Manhood. It's a rite of passage honoring your cadets for their efforts during the tasks. More than anything it's a great time to bond with your children. It also can serve as a final exam pulling together all the skills developed over the course of the missions.

The Components of the Celebration

We offer this guide as a suggestion of events modify and add your own ideas. The celebration need not cost hundreds of dollars or require weeks of planning.

Location for the Celebration

It seems most appropriate that the Missions to Manhood be celebrated outside at a campground, a park, the wilderness or the arctic tundra. Operation Bugout is a perfect setup for the celebration. If you have the means to head off the beaten path then more power to you. The goal is that the location is somewhere special apart from the cadets regular routine.

Ceremonial Gifts for Boys

A token presented to the kids at the completion of the missions provides a unique way to honor their discipline and efforts while providing a keepsake for them to treasure.

Summing up the spirit of the missions it can be useful, uniquely manly, maybe a bit dangerous and ideally engraved or personalized for the child. The gift need not be expensive to meet these requirements, but it shouldn't be an everyday item. Ideas: high-quality knife, tactical flashlight, a multi-tool, a unique hand tool, a watch, a fishing pole. Engraving by laser or traditional methods will make the gift even more special.

Celebration of Man Activities

In keeping with the spirit of the missions use your time to do some unique activities. Throw knives, shoot BB guns, go to a rifle range, cook over a fire, play poker, throw rocks at targets, go fishing, go hunting, have Airsoft battles, go orienteering. Other ideas could include a multi-stage scavenger hunt. Have an outdoor cooking contest.

The Actual Celebration of Man

One scenario: you have gathered around a fire that the cadet started with their fire steel, have finished an authentic camp meal and you're ready to celebrate.

Suggested order of events:

» Review their Man Points earned during the missions.

» Talk about mission highlights, what was their favorite?

» Discuss what skills they learned. What mission was most difficult?

» Share your favorite moments from the various missions.

» Provide feedback to your cadet about growth you've witnessed during this time.

» Reinforce your commitment to being there for them on their journey to manhood.

» Present them with their gifts.

After Action Report

We celebrated while camping Operation Bugout style. As was previously mentioned wildfire had severely burned the area but in no way dampened our spirits. We journeyed into the hills to throw knives and ninja stars. We ate questionable food around the campfire. During the evening we talked through the missions, and the boys received their gifts. They each received a Zero Tolerance assisted pocket knife with their name laser engraved on the blade.

CHAPTER 4

Mission Overview

Consider this chapter the parents workbook for each mission. Cadets if you're reading this, move to your guide! For each of the tasks, you'll find a list of recommended resources. Each mission includes caveats and insight for the commanding officer based on our own experience and lessons learned running the tasks. Finally, you'll see mission feedback from our own boys which I call the after action report.

Printable Mission Guides

If you'd like to have a printed mission guide for your cadet https://journeytomen.com/downloads will provide options including the ability to purchase letter sized formatted PDF documents. Located at the same webpage you'll find blank documents to download for the missions that require tracking information such as Operation Penny Pinch and Operation Time Crisis.

If you're reading the eBook version of Journey to Men I would highly recommend purchasing the formatted Mission Guides for your cadet, they are visually pleasing and in many cases your child will need to refer back to the guide for more information.

Mission 1: Operation Timbuktu

Navigate a Mechanized Vehicle to a Fixed Way Point

Picture this scenario: you take a right turn onto the street intersecting with your home's driveway and your child from the back seat asks, "how long until we're home?" Does this sound familiar? Do yourself and your kids a favor and give them a taste of being in charge while they navigate you to a specific location. There's no real downside to failure with these missions unless they navigate you into a bridge abutment and you follow their directions. Have fun with it, let them enjoy the independence and maybe even a little frustration along the way. That's okay, life is often frustrating.

Mission Synopsis

Your mission is to navigate your C.O.'s (parental unit) vehicle to a location of your mutual choosing and the return trip to command H.Q. This location should be outside the scope of your regular daily travels such as a restaurant, army surplus store, break dancing academy or the like. Technology use is appropriate for the route planning portion of the assignment only.

Resources

Mission notebook, a pen or pencil, access to a computer or device for research on https://www.google.com/maps or similar mapping site.

Caveats

Make this destination a location outside of the normal daily routine. Perhaps a cool restaurant, to see a movie or a store they've always wanted to visit. And unless the situation is dire, dutifully follow their navigation.

After Action Report

I wrote this mission expressly for my 11-year-old who would frequently look out the window and say, "where are we?" Me: "We're on the same road we've travelled for the last 9 years." Our boys loved this mission for the freedom it afforded them to choose their own destination. Many other participant families let all the kids in the family take a turn as a navigator. This is a great mission to repeat, see Operation Time Crisis for additional practice opportunities coupled with time management skills.

Mission 2. Operation Metaknife

Learn Knife Skills and Whittle a Letter Opener

Parents if you only choose one thing to do with your kids from Journey to Men, get them a pocket knife and let them use it. You are telling your boys you trust them and they'll feel immeasurable pride in their fantastic tool. The Victorinox Swiss Army Huntsman Pocket Knife is the model we recommend. It's well made and has a variety of tools useful for many common tasks.

Mission Synopsis

Your mission is to familiarize yourself with your everyday carry tool and to use it to whittle a wood knife letter opener or similar project.

Resources

Your cadet will need a pocket knife, their mission notebook, pen or pencil and some form of wood. For the wood, encourage them to look around their home environment to make the knife, as a last resort you can purchase some lumber building materials. The mission covers what types of materials to look for.

Caveats

Yes, knives can be dangerous. Age ranges here are at your discretion, my boys were ages 11 and 13 when they completed this mission, but they'd been using knives since they were 8. It might be in your best interest to supervise their initial knife work to make sure safety is being practiced. Before any carving, the cadet should read through the mission and the special addendum on knife usage.

After Action Report

This is a wonderful mission to spur creativity, include a

little danger and learn some knife skills. We received many pictures of completed metaknives using myriad materials. Whittling seems like an old pastime, but I thoroughly believe this to be a timeless pursuit especially suitable for sitting around a campfire. Combine this mission with Operation Pack Mule and Operation Inferno, and you've got the makings for an excellent camping trip.

Mission 3: Operation Good Neighbor

Help a Neighbor in Need

As part of the lessons both my wife and I are trying to teach our kids, we've long focused on helping others. The Missus is much better at this than I am, on any given week you'll see the boys tagging along with her to visit someone in poor health or a person who needs some assistance. One day we were driving home, and we passed an injured biker on the side of the road, so we stopped to check on his condition. My son said later "I'm happy that we are the kind of people who would stop and help someone in trouble." That's powerful stuff both for you and them. This mission puts a little more focus on the kids initiating the help and I daresay is one of the most important of the 25 Missions to Manhood.

Mission Synopsis

This mission is simple but important. Being a good neighbor is not just a mission; it should be a way of life. If your neighbors can't count on those around them to help in a time of need, who can they rely on? It's known as the Golden Rule and is one of the most important things you can learn. It's this: Love Your Neighbor as Yourself. What does that mean? It means you should treat others how you want to be treated and love them even when it might be difficult or not particularly enjoyable. You'll go find a neighbor (one you think might most need the help) and go offer your support and assistance. Then you will provide whatever help they need or figure out how to get it to them.

Resources

The necessary supplies will entirely depend on the help required, like a lawnmower, shovels, a book to read with the neighbor.

Caveats

Operation Good Neighbor is foremost a lesson in service and giving. It might be challenging for your child to complete this mission on their own, but as in all the missions, we encourage you to have them try.

After Action Report

Our two boys are very different, and at this stage in their young lives, they interacted very differently with adults. The oldest had no issues talking to or relating to older people, and he would do fine just visiting with neighbors. Our middle son was hesitant to interact with adults and needed encouragement to do so. For him, the services he could offer were more in line with physical work such as lawn mowing. The time spent helping others at a young age has gone a long way to shape the young men they are becoming. That same middle son, now in high school used one of his elective classes to tutor special education classmates.

Mission 4: Operation Inferno

Build and Start a Fire

Fire building is a classic camping activity but works just as well out in the backyard fire pit. There's a good chance your young cadet has dabbled with building a fire but we're going to kick it up a notch by using firesteel and making some firestarters using cotton balls and petroleum jelly. Your boys (and girls) will love the process, especially working with the firesteel. Is it totally necessary? No. Is it great fun and a way to feel really manly? You bet.

Mission Synopsis

Creating fire is an essential skill for wilderness survival, cooking and roasting marshmallows. In this mission, we'll assemble the equipment and materials necessary to build a fire outdoors using Swedish firesteel and a great firestarter product created from cotton balls and Vaseline or petroleum jelly. As always we'll do this very safely.

Resources

Swedish firesteel or Ferro rod, cotton balls, and petroleum jelly. If you're searching for a brand of firesteel, the UCO Light My Fire Mini Swedish Firesteel is an excellent choice. It comes with a small scraper that you drag down the steel to create the spark. This is superior to using a pocket knife for obvious safety reasons. It is readily available in sporting and outdoor stores as well as online.

Caveats

Like many of our missions, there is a concern of safety, so supervision is essential. While we try to provide some guidance on making a fire safely in our Mission Guide, we can't cover all potential safety scenarios. Also, beware of burn bans which always seem to crop up in our popular campsites during the end of summer.

After Action Report

Of all the missions in Journey to Men, this one, in particular, had staying power all summer. At any given time the boys would be attempting to start a fire using their firesteel and exotic firestarters. The dryer lint gathered from Operation Skidmark makes for an excellent firestarter material as well.

Mission 5: Operation Packmule

Ready Your Gear for Travel and Load Vehicle

Packing the vehicle has always been my job. I learned the fine art from my own father. Honestly it's probably because the process of fitting the puzzle pieces of luggage and equipment into a tight space is a satisfying experience for my logical brain. Not to mention that way I wasn't dealing with the pandemonium inside the house trying to get the boys ready to leave. This mission is an attempt to pass on those skills and responsibility to the next generation of quartermasters.

Mission Synopsis

When readying for any trip or adventure outfitting yourself with the proper equipment is critical. In this mission, you will prepare for an upcoming trip or vacation by gathering your gear. Further, if this trip requires vehicle travel, you'll help assemble the rest of the squad's gear and pack it efficiently and effectively.

Resources

Bag or suitcase for stowing your gear (never a garbage bag). Gear to go in your bag. Packing list from mission guide.

Caveats

It's hard as parents not to intervene while your kids are packing. Unless it's a life and death situation involving medication or hypothermia, we're strongly suggesting that you don't intervene in the process. If they follow the packing list, they will probably pack more than they would have otherwise brought in the first place.

After Action Report

We ran this mission before our niece's high school graduation, and we stuck to the mission parameters with zero supervision. One boy forgot to bring along his dress pants, so he attended the ceremony wearing his dress shirt and basketball shorts. That was a lesson he has never forgotten. From that moment on they were responsible for assembling their own gear for better or worse. It never ceases to amaze me how they can provide three days of clothing in a small duffel bag.

Mission 6: Operation Pennypinch

Saving for a Big Ticket Item

Personal finance is an area where a lot of adults lack confidence let alone kids. How powerful would it be if you helped your child avoid some financial mistakes you have made? Mastering the habit of delayed gratification is difficult but we'll focus on one simple goal, saving for a reward. This is the goal of Operation Pennypinch.

Mission Synopsis

In this mission you'll identify a big ticket item (maybe in the $100-200 range), make a savings plan and track your progress to your goal. Working with your commanding officer (C.O.) you might also explore opening a bank account.

Resources

Savings goal sheet provided at the end of the mission document, mission notebook.

Caveats

This could evolve into a complicated lesson teaching kids about personal finance, but the ultimate aim of this mission is to focus on the discipline of saving money and hitting a goal. Operation Kickstart (mission 10) will have them explore ways to generate income to hit their savings target.

After Action Report

Our own kids are very different in many things including their approach to money. Our younger boy will look for ways to spend whatever surplus income comes his way while our older son will just happily sock his money away. They weren't particularly successful with the first draft of this mission while feedback from other cadets showed them navigating to their favorite store (Operation Timbuktu style) to purchase the item for which they had been diligently saving.

Mission 7: Operation Rise and Shine

Prepare Breakfast for Your Squad

Cooking breakfast is an excellent activity for your kids and a variety of ages can tackle this task thanks to the simplicity of the meal. This mission requires a little more guidance from the commanding officer to make sure they are being safe and to provide training on the more complicated kitchen tools.

Mission Synopsis

Preparing a meal for yourself and others is a vital skill for any cadet. Breakfast is a great place to start your cooking adventure as you can choose various foods and recipes as your skills develop. Your mission is to feed your squad breakfast and includes: planning a breakfast menu, shopping for ingredients, cooking the meal and cleaning.

Resources

Ingredients for your meal such as eggs, bread, cereal, juice, pans and cooking implements, a kitchen.

Caveats

With all the missions, safety is a significant concern especially if this a new endeavor for your cadet. The mission guide does not detail all the hazards of working with stoves, ovens, knives, mixers, that instruction falls to the C.O. before the mission begins. A suggestion is to have a safety briefing with all members of the squad taking part in the meal preparation, so they have the best opportunity for success. It will also be necessary to give them their mission ahead of time to make their list and shop.

After Action Report

Our boys enjoyed this mission apart from the cleanup process. They chose a morning while we were on vacation with our family friends and all the kids took part. It is still a tradition every mothers day for them to prepare a menu and cook breakfast to honor their Mom. Their menu is always titled Ixtapa after their beloved hometown Mexican restaurant.

Mission 8: Operation Brokenspoke

Overhaul and Maintain Your Bicycle

This mission assumes that the kids have a bike which may or may not be a reality. In the same vein, they could apply this mission to any form of vehicle they may own such as a scooter, skateboard, big wheel or hoverboard. The real goal of this mission is for them to think about their gear in a different light and develop some respect for the things they own, and the value of keeping it in operating condition.

Mission Synopsis

Your mission is to clean, lubricate, inspect and if necessary repair your two-wheeler. Keeping your vehicles in good working order is vital to field exercises like running to the store or escaping a roving biker gang.

Resources

Bicycle or another vehicle, hose, bucket, car wash soap, sponge or wash mitt, towel, Simple Green cleaner or similar, brush (tooth or other), rag, lubricant, bike multi-tool, wrenches.

Caveats

This mission is heavy on resource requirements especially if bike repair is necessary. You might recommend that your cadet focuses on some aspects such as cleaning if you think it's too involved for them. As with all missions if this isn't appropriate for your situation feel free to move on to the next task.

After Action Report

This mission resonated with the boys and they were out first thing in the morning getting their bikes clean and lubricated. My son's best friend rolled down the street to get in the action as well. For some extra man points, you can always direct them towards the family vehicle.

Mission 9: Operation Gas Pumper

Fuel the Squad Transport

Pumping gas is a common vehicle maintenance task that is very approachable for children and makes an excellent mission and ongoing chore. It also will make them feel pretty darn important.

Mission Synopsis

Keeping your vehicle operational and ready to roll is a critical component of your journey to being men. In this mission, you'll fuel your squad's car and do a spot safety check to make sure your rig is safe for the road.

Resources

A vehicle, you're C.O.'s payment source.

Caveats

The mission parameters warn the cadet to be safe when pumping gas, by touching the side of their vehicle when getting out to go pump the gas. As always a quick safety briefing by the C.O. can help for the first time gas pumper, but they can have plenty of opportunities to practice this task.

After Action Report

This quickly became one of my wife's favorite missions as she could send the boys out in the rain to top off the wagon. Funny story, we lived in Washington for most of the boys younger lives and would travel to Oregon frequently where an attendant pumped your gasoline. I can still picture the look of disgust on my boy's faces when they learned that they could not pump gas in their own vehicle.

Mission 10: Operation Kickstart

Start a Kid Small Business

I think back fondly at those simple kid jobs I performed in our neighborhood. With my neighbor Max we'd roll the lawnmower down the street headed to our various jobs. Sure mowing over dog poop and having it sprayed in your face is pretty terrible but you'll learn to be more thorough picking up the dog poop before you start mowing next time! In this mission, your kid will develop their own business idea and execute their simple business plan. They'll find a list of kid business ideas to help get the creative juices flowing.

Mission Synopsis

In Operation Pennypinch you set a savings target, now in Operation Kickstart, you'll start a small business to earn money towards your goal. A kid business should be simple, use one of our ideas or come up with your own and you'll be bringing in money in no time.

Resources

Mission notebook, whatever materials your business may require.

Caveats

An essential step of Operation Kickstart is developing a business plan or strategy. Obviously, your guidance in viable business ideas is helpful for their success. If you live in the middle of nowhere an ice cream stand might not be very effective, nor would snow blowing driveways be particularly lucrative during the summer months.

After Action Report

Life skills come quickly when you're running your own business. Our own kids learned the value of thinking through pricing structures so they didn't work for pennies. While I contemplated intervening with the neighbor about wage renegotiation for a job that required many more hours than planned, pushing our boy to complete his agreed-upon task was much more important for his character.

Mission 11: Operation Condor

Build a birdhouse

Building a birdhouse is a great beginning woodworking project suitable for a wide age range. The mission briefing provides just enough information to kick off the building process while not detailing every build step. A large part of the Journey to Men missions is an attempt to get the kids thinking and problem-solving. The birds don't care if their house is ugly.

Mission Synopsis

Your mission is to build a birdhouse. This birdhouse should not be for a condor as a condor is the largest flying bird in North America also known as a vulture. Operation Condor just sounds cooler than Operation Tufted Titmouse. A birdhouse is a classic woodworking project and a great place to start your carpentry career. This house will provide an excellent place for your winged friends to live and also makes a great item to sell for Operation Kickstart.

Resources

Mission notebook, cedar fence boards 1x4x6 and 1x6x6 or similar, miter box, saw, drill, 1 1/2" drill bit, hammer, 6D Galvanized nails, tape measure, pencil, and square. Perch material like a branch, golf tee or dowel, safety glasses.

Caveats

Since this project involves tools, there is some element of danger, supervision might be necessary depending on your child and their age. This is a straightforward mission that requires creativity and critical thinking. Resist the urge to buy one of the prepackaged birdhouse kits available at big box home improvement stores so that your cadet will create something truly unique.

After Action Report

A building project such as this mission will often inspire your kids in different ways. Our two boys approached this project very differently. The older spent a fair amount of time designing his project on paper while our middle son just started cutting. They were busy working on this project for the better part of a weekend as they also decided to do some painting. Great fun was had by all.

Mission 12: Operation Clean Sweep

Ready and Clean Your Living Quarters

Since the dawn of mankind, kids have avoided cleaning their room. Operation Clean Sweep presents a phased approach to clean an area in stages. With the added motivation of some Man Points perhaps you'll see a change in attitude.

Mission Synopsis

As a cadet that's part of a larger family squad, it's your duty to clean up after yourself, simple as that. Your mission is to clean your primary living areas such as your bedroom, TV room, kitchen, bathroom or wherever you spend some time.

Resources

Household cleaning equipment, vacuum, broom, dusting materials, bathroom cleaners, garbage bag.

Caveats

This might be the most challenging mission your cadet will undertake. Most children will find little novelty in the cleaning process, I get it. It's very tempting to let the kids off easy, no discipline seems easy at the time. There's a reason this mission is in place between Operation Condor and Operation Knot my Job to balance the fun with duty.

After Action Report

When our boys performed this mission initially, it was the first time in the history of their lives that they cleaned a room, actually clean without multiple checks. Another squad renamed this mission "Operation Weep and Sweep," which might be a more appropriate mission title.

Mission 13: Operation Knot My Job

Knot Tying in the Heat of Battle

Knot tying is a useful skill whether you're out on the water, securing a tarp over a load destined for the landfill or putting up a badminton net in the backyard. While your cadet is working on their knot tying skills, they'll have some fun along the way.

Mission Synopsis

Knot tying is an important skill that is often overlooked, but as you'll see in this mission, it just might save your life!

Resources

Paracord or similar rope approximately 20 feet in length, a tree branch or pipe, tarp.

Caveats

This is a straightforward mission that is easy to modify to put additional man points on the tally sheet. Do you spend a lot of time on the water, have your child practice some basic mooring knots. If your cadet is having trouble tying the knots reference, the excellent website: https://www.animatedknots.com/ for a detailed look at the knot tying process. For all participants using rope of a thicker nature will make the whole knot tying process easier.

After Action Report

Our two boys loved working on the knots and found it useful in some other missions including the MacGyver challenge. Bonus points if you simulate the biker gang by riding your bike through their trap!

Mission 14: Operation Avocation

Research and Develop a New Hobby

If you aren't in a phase of your parenting journey where every waking moment of your kids existence revolves around their screens this mission might not seem as novel as the others. If on the other hand, you're continually trying to pry the tablet out of your youngster's hands then this task is an excellent way to help them broaden their horizons.

Mission Synopsis

After a reconnaissance mission to your local library, your mission is to research, choose and explore a new hobby or pastime.

Resources

A library card (you can get one at the library if you don't already have one), your mission notebook and whatever you might need for your new hobby.

Caveats

Full disclosure your author is a serial hobbyist. I spent most of my childhood building models, constructing forts, boomerang crafting, and RC car racing. The Journey to Men book is a result of my desire to try something new. I meant this mission to inspire some curiosity and creativity, and the hope is your child will find something new and exciting to try.

In the mission guide your cadet will find a list of potential hobbies but by no means is this an exhaustive resource. If you enjoy a particular hobby, but you have not introduced it to your child, this might be a great time.

After Action Report

Over the years the kids have tried any number of hobbies such as Pokemon card collecting, magic, martial arts, knife throwing, Airsoft along with other more traditional sports. In the pursuit of those hobbies, it exposed them to diverse points of view and people they might not have otherwise had the opportunity to meet.

Mission 15: Operation Perseverance

Design and Keep a Physical Fitness Goal

Kids, adults it doesn't matter, most every study suggests that we need to be moving and exercising more. In most pursuits, the practice of self-discipline will turn your ideas into reality. The choice of activity or plan matters much less than the actual implementation and adherence.

Mission Synopsis

Your mission is to set a goal to do some form of physical fitness every day for 30 days. Exercise is a necessary part of anyone's well being and setting goals and achieving them are important lessons for life.

Resources

Whatever you might need to perform your exercise, perhaps a ball, stick and pucks, your mission notebook.

Caveats

If you've spent any time in a corporate environment or listened to leadership podcasts, you've probably heard of a SMART goal. SMART stands for Specific, Measurable, Achievable, Relevant and Time-bound. This is the perfect mechanism for helping your young cadet reach their goals. By setting up their exercise goal which is achievable in a specific time-frame they'll gain a heap of confidence. While we have repeatedly warned about being too prescriptive during your child's mission, time spent planning with them will be most helpful for their success.

After Action Report

This mission is a tall order indeed and depending on your child's personality might be surprisingly challenging or relatively straightforward. Our own children we have learned later in life deal with attention deficit disorder and hyperactivity, respectively. As it turns out the hyperactive child had no issue with some form of daily exercise and in fact required it for his well being. My older son who struggles with ADD found this mission to be incredibly challenging, like most things in his life that requires constant diligence. The best recommendation is to make this a fun mission and give them plenty of encouragement along the way. Avoid nagging or prompting them to perform their daily task. This is their mission after all.

Mission 16: Operation Wheels on the Bus

Utilize Public Transport to Reach a Destination

We lived in a rural area neighboring on larger cities. The bus service in our neighborhood consisted of one route to get to the main bus transfer station which is quite comprehensive, it just takes some time and understanding to reach the terminal. As such, our boys had never ridden public transportation. This mission is as challenging for the boys as it is for the parental units letting them complete the mission.

Mission Synopsis

In our original mission Operation Timbuktu, you navigated a mechanized vehicle to a destination. In Operation Wheels On The Bus, you'll use some of your navigation skills to ride public transport to a destination.

Resources

Computer or bus route maps, mission notebook, phone for communication to H.Q.

Caveats

As in all missions, safety is of paramount importance, and if you decide that this mission is inappropriate for your child based on their age, environment, availability of public transport or any other factor move to the next task. A further recommendation would be to send your cadet with a buddy or family member.

After Action Report

Our boys were ages 11 and 13 when they first completed this mission. Because we were living in such a rural area, we did not fear for their safety, and they thoroughly enjoyed traveling without their C.O.'s present.

Mission 17: The MacGyver Challenge

Save the Village from Noxious Gas Ants

This is a fun mission that challenges the cadets to use their creativity and critical thinking skills to develop a mechanism to drop the serum (an egg) safely from 6 feet or higher. You may not be familiar with MacGyver, you can find the original TV show starring Richard Dean Anderson on Amazon Prime Video and other online sources. It's particularly relevant for boys working through Journey to Men. You'll never see MacGyver without his swiss army knife, and in each show, he's in some predicament that requires him to figure a way out using only materials available around him. This mission is a tribute to the beloved show.

Mission Synopsis

An enormous colony of a previously undiscovered Egyptian Gas Ant has infested your village of Journeyton, and you're being called in to save the day. You parachute into the infectious disease lab only to find it's exposed to the deadly gas except for a small room and a deck outside the lab. You must get the serum safely to the National Guard who is waiting below your building but how will you do it in time with only 60 minutes and the supplies you've found in the closet?

Resources

Swiss Army Knife, eggs and various building materials. This is up to the C.O. to determine the resources available during the mission. Some sample items: Gorilla Tape, tongue depressors, gauze bandages, paracord, bendy straws.

Caveats

You might find it hard not to provide guidance or suggestions as they are working on their serum holding mechanism, resist the urge! It's also highly suggested that you have extra materials and eggs on hand so they can experiment and try multiple times. For our challenge we simulated them being locked in a closet with first aid equipment and food supplies. Just have fun with this mission, and it's a great one to involve friends, family, neighbors.

After Action Report

We ran this mission on vacation with some close family friends, all four kids were simultaneously building their serum holders. Our friends found it exceedingly difficult not to provide unsolicited coaching during the build process. We had a survival rate of 3 of the 4 eggs, one cracked during the build process. We spent the better part of the day devising new contraptions both adults and kids alike.

Mission 18: Operation Falling Water

Build a Water Balloon Launcher

Launching water balloons great distances is an excellent way to spend a summer day, even better when your kids have built their water balloon launcher themselves.

Mission Synopsis

Your mission is to construct a device suitable for launching water balloons over long distances. Directions cover building our model but feel free to improvise and implement your own designs.

Resources

4 feet of surgical tubing or exercise bands or polespear rubber tubing, duct tape (Gorilla tape strongly recommended), towel or tarp or other heavy fabric approximately 15"x15", 5/8" dowel or scrap of wood approximately 18" long, saw, scissors, water balloons.

Caveats

The real challenge for this mission parents is finding surgical tubing for the launcher. As we've stated in the equipment section, online might be the easiest but sporting good stores with a good fishing department are also good sources for tubing. We personally used Spearit 3/8in OD 3/16in ID Polespear Band/Sling Thick Walled Latex Rubber Tubing ONE Continuous Piece(#606) from Amazon, and it worked really well. Safety is also a concern here if the tubing snaps your cadet in the face it's going to leave a severe welt, not to mention potential for eye damage. Safety glasses are a must!

After Action Report

Our kids loved this mission, it was a craft project they could really get behind. You can add to this mission by setting up targets to knock down. If they don't have another squad member around they can improvise a base to mount the launcher to for one person launching.

Mission 19: Operation Correspondence

Write a Letter to a Relative

Letter writing is a skill that is severely waning in popularity, but short of an in-person visit what better way to convey your thoughtfulness? Letter writing for boys might seem like a form of torture, but when they see the impact that it has on their loved ones, they will probably change their mind. What's manly about writing a letter? Caring for people you love is extremely masculine, and a handwritten note will help them know someone loves them.

Mission Synopsis

If you can't be with your beloved Grandmother in person few things will mean as much to her as a handwritten letter from one of her favorite people in the world, you. In this mission, you'll write a properly formatted letter and send it to someone you love.

Resources

Stationery for the letter, pen, envelope, stamp.

Caveats

This is a straightforward mission, and while it might not be your cadets most favorite action-packed task, this is an excellent character building exercise. Perhaps your child enjoys our break dance sample letter, and you could help them create or find a unique set of stationery of their very own.

After Action Report

Our kids are typical, and this was no easy task to complete even as the first Journey to Men official cadets. We had to remind our boys this task isn't for you, it's for your loved one. One of the key traits we try to instill in our kids is a focus to think about and care for others. If their loved ones are like ours, they'll hear all about what a difference that letter made in their day, and they just might get a letter back in return.

Mission 20: Operation Foxhole

Dig a Fighting Hole to Survive a Frontal Assault

Digging a hole is a classic boy activity that we fully embrace here at Journey to Men. There will be no shortage of physical labor in this challenge, add the impending frontal assault and they'll have ample motivation to dig a foxhole quickly.

Mission Synopsis

The military has used foxholes in warfare since World War I to protect soldiers from gunfire, artillery, tanks, and other dangers. Your mission is to dig an entrenchment that will allow you to survive a frontal assault by your C.O. or other attackers.

Resources

Entrenching tool or shovel, defensive weaponry (optional), suitable foxhole digging area.

Caveats

Locating a suitable site for your child to dig the foxhole might be the first challenge. A strong suggestion is to set a deadline that the "attack" will occur. Your job is to provide the frontal assault to test the suitability of your cadet's defenses. You could launch your attack with the help of Nerf guns, a hose, Airsoft weapons or other options. The knowledge that an attack is imminent provides all the necessary motivation.

After Action Report

Our kids loved this mission and completed it with the help of their visiting cousin. We'd never witnessed our kids work harder than Operation Foxhole as they knew that the enemy forces would be landing at 5:30pm after they got off work. They quite successfully fended off the invading marauders who attacked with Airsoft guns and in the end drove them off.

Mission 21: Operation Time Crisis

Manage Your Teams Time Schedule and Save the Town

Time management is a skill that requires practice to master. This mission turns over the control of an entire day to your cadet to help them understand the dependencies of not only themselves but others in their immediate family.

Mission Synopsis

Bad news cadet, there has been a re-infestation of Egyptian gas ants in your neighboring town. The department of civilian health is trucking in a critical shipment of antidote to your location, but due to the explosive nature of the serum, it has to be received precisely at the stated time to its shipment location. Your assignment is to schedule your local squad's schedule for the day being sure to meet the shipment on time at the specified location.

Resources

Some form of timekeeping device: a wristwatch, an atomic clock, sundial. Mission notebook and a writing instrument.

Caveats

The challenge for this task is finding a day that you can entirely turn over to your cadet to manage. Mission planning must begin prior to the task day allowing the cadet ample time to develop the squad schedule. As with the other tasks resist the urge to correct them throughout the day and let them have the freedom to succeed or fail on their own merit. Make sure to provide a specific time for the serum delivery for their scheduling.

After Action Report

Time management is a real challenge around our household. With three kids all involved in sports, school and church activities it takes serious planning to get them where they need to be every day. As I'm writing this my oldest boy has snoozed his alarm clock no less than 4 times. This mission was not a part of our trial run, and as such, we haven't received feedback from the field. If you found this mission fun, challenging, impossible, we'd love to know. As always we welcome you to update us at paul@journeytomen.com.

Mission 22: Operation Safehouse

Build an Emergency Shelter

Practicing survival skills while having fun is the name of the game with Operation Safehouse. Your job as the C.O. is to test the sturdiness of their shelter using a variety of means, see the Mission parameters for more complete details. This is a perfect mission to run if you are camping perhaps while you are having the Celebration of Man?

Mission Synopsis

In a survival situation shelter is a critical component that can mean the difference between life or death. Your mission is to build a shelter that is big enough for you to lie down inside comfortably and that will protect you from your local dangers such as wind, rain, animals, and marauders.

Resources

Your pocket knife, paracord (perhaps from a survival bracelet), a water bottle.

Caveats

Read through the mission guide with your cadet and you can decide what tests are feasible based on where you run this mission.

After Action Report

My boys required zero motivation to complete this mission. The boys especially enjoyed the "testing" of the shelter. With the first iteration of their shelters, they quickly discovered they were unsuitable for lasting an entire night. Root balls will do that. Later they worked together to make a larger tarp structure that they then slept in multiple times throughout the summer.

Mission 23: Operation Blowout

Replace a Tire on a Mechanized Vehicle

This mission requires an experienced cadet and might not be suitable for younger kids. We can't stress enough the importance of proper supervision to ensure the safety of all squad members. One of the most enjoyable aspects of Operation Blowout is watching your cadet try to locate the spare tire with newer vehicles the engineers have become more and more creative and/or cruel depending on your point of view.

Mission Synopsis

Your maintenance unit is responding to a reported flat tire on your squad's personnel carrier. You are to locate the spare tire and tools necessary for changing the tire and perform a tire change. NOTE: YOUR C.O. MUST SUPERVISE ALL ASPECTS OF THIS MISSION! BE SAFE!

Resources

Vehicle, spare tire, jack, lug wrench, blocks for wheels, screwdriver.

Caveats

Did we mention the importance of safety? If you don't have a car or your vehicle happens to be one of the unfortunate newer models that does not include a spare different accommodations are required, perhaps another family member can help. For your own safety as well as your cadets you will, of course, want to ensure that they tighten the lug nuts fully.

After Action Report

I ran a test on our oldest boy to see if he could locate the spare tire on the truck that he drives to school every day. He was at first skeptical that there was actually a spare located somewhere on the vehicle. When he realized that it was underneath the bed of the truck in the rear his mind was blown.

Mission 24: Operation Bugout

Embark on an Overnight Outdoor Deployment

This is a large scale mission that will tax your cadet's capabilities. As you read further about the Celebration of Man, this is an excellent task to run in parallel with that event. Your child will have the opportunity to demonstrate a whole host of their skills including navigation, packing, food preparation, camp setup and of course clean up.

Mission Synopsis

Using the considerable skills you've developed throughout your previous missions you are to take your C.O. and squad on an outdoor overnight trip. As the acting field commander for this deployment, you will need to plan all logistics for the journey including location reconnaissance, meal planning, housing preparation and keeping your squad alive.

Resources

Mission notebook, pen or pencil, maps or internet access for mission prep, recipes, food, camping equipment, clothing, first aid kit.

Caveats

This mission assumes that camping is feasible in your environment and that, of course, might not be an accurate assessment. You could just as easily alter this mission for most any destination like a hotel or Grandma's house. You might also want to sneak some beef jerky along so you'll have something to eat in the case of food prep mishaps.

After Action Report

This was an incredibly memorable family trip for so many reasons starting with our arrival at a campsite that only had just opened that weekend after a massive wildfire. It looked as if we were camping on a scorched moon, but there were no crowds to speak of. The boys also undertook an ambitious menu that included deep-fried wings over the camp stove. Fortunately, any combustible materials in the campsite had previously burned in the wildfire as mentioned earlier. Some wings were edible, so we didn't starve. The trip in no way proceeded as we expected, but we frequently reminisce about all the things that went wrong and how much fun we had doing it together.

Mission 25: Operation Skidmark

Perform Laundry Operations

Let's not tap dance around the obvious here, laundry is not fun. That being said it's an important skill and put in the context of Missions to Manhood is much more palatable than a standard Saturday morning.

Mission Synopsis

Your stockpile of clean clothes is running low cadet get them to the washer before you have to call in a fast mover to destroy whatever is growing in your laundry hamper.

Resources

Washer, Dryer, laundry detergent, dirty laundry, laundry basket.

Caveats

It is understood that some feel strongly about laundry and the proper methods of performing the laundry process. If that describes you or your significant other, we encourage you to pass on your washing expertise to your cadet and let them do their own laundry.

After Action Report

Our cadets have been doing their own laundry for years. Early in our family life we quickly determined that no one enjoyed doing laundry and as such we each are responsible for our own loads. As they have gotten older and riper they have learned to value the laundry process overall.

CHAPTER 5

Mission Point Tally

On the following page is a prepared table listing the 25 missions with minimum and maximum "man point" possibilities. As I mentioned earlier in the Parent Guide, the point system is a simple tracking tool that is optional depending on the participants. The minimum point total is what the cadet can earn if they perform the base mission components. If the cadet was to complete the entire mission and the extra credit, they would earn the maximum points denoted by this column.

The original 25 mission concept assumes you will run all missions together, for instance, during a summer break. Feel free to segment the missions into smaller blocks suitable for school vacations or long weekends. In that mission cluster scenario you can provide a small prize once they complete the tasks. There is no reason not to change the mission schedule to suit your squad's needs.

	MISSION	MIN	MAX
1	Operation Timbuktu	1000	1100
2	Operation Metaknife	1000	1100
3	Operation Good Neighbor	1000	2000
4	Operation Inferno	500	1000
5	Operation Packmule	1500	1600
6	Operation Pennypinch	750	1750
7	Operation Rise and Shine	500	1500
8	Operation Brokenspoke	1000	1250
9	Operation Gas Pumper	1000	1000
10	Operation Kickstart	1250	5250
11	Operation Condor	1000	2000
12	Operation Cleansweep	1000	5000
13	Operation Knot My Job	1000	2000
14	Operation Avocation	500	1000
15	Operation Perseverance	500	3250
16	Operation Wheels on the Bus	1000	2500
17	The Macgyver Challenge	1000	2000
18	Operation Falling Water	1000	1000
19	Operation Correspondence	1000	2000
20	Operation Foxhole	1000	2250
21	Operation Time Crisis	1000	4000
22	Operation Safe House	1500	3000
23	Operation Blowout	3000	3000
24	Operation Bugout	1500	2000
25	Operation Skidmark	2500	2500
	TOTALS	**28,000**	**55,050**

Suggested Man Point Targets

One question that is frequently asked is how many
Man Points does my child need to qualify for the Celebration
of Man? The response is always the same, it depends. A safe
number assuming you will complete all the 25 missions is
to use the standard point total which is 28,000 points. If
you are encouraging your cadet to achieve more than the
baseline points, you can pick a larger number with additional
incentives. As I previously suggested, these targets should
be communicated at the outset of the missions so that your
child is not trying to hit a moving target. Obviously the goal
is that all participants are successful even if they are taking
part differently.

CHAPTER 6

Feedback Requested

Book Review

I hope you have enjoyed Journey to Men and the 25 Missions to Manhood. If you would like to pass on your appreciation you can do that through whatever store you purchased this book via their review system. It helps so much, thank you!

Mission Pictures and Feedback

One of the highlights for me and other participants of Journey to Men is seeing other cadets and their C.O's actively performing their missions. If you'd like to share in your Journey you can do that a variety of ways. You can reach me always at paul@journeytomen.com or through the Contact form on the website https://journeytomen.com.

Facebook

Join a community of Journey to Men participants at our Facebook page by liking and following us at: https://www.facebook.com/journeytomen/.

Instagram

If you're comfortable sharing your mission pictures to the internet at large tag us @journeytomen on Instagram and include hashtag #journeytomen.

KID

GUIDE

Missions

KNIFE GUIDE 74

OPERATION TIMBUKTU 77

OPERATION METAKNIFE 81

OPERATION GOOD NEIGHBOR. 85

OPERATION INFERNO 89

OPERATION PACKMULE. 95

OPERATION PENNYPINCH 101

OPERATION RISE AND SHINE 107

OPERATION BROKENSPOKE 113

OPERATION GAS PUMPER. 119

OPERATION KICKSTART. 125

OPERATION CONDOR. 131

OPERATION CLEANSWEEP 137

OPERATION KNOT MY JOB 143

OPERATION AVOCATION. 149

OPERATION PERSEVERANCE 155

OPERATION WHEELS ON THE BUS 159

THE MACGYVER CHALLENGE. 165

OPERATION FALLING WATER. 169

OPERATION CORRESPONDENCE 175

OPERATION FOXHOLE 181

OPERATION TIME CRISIS. 187

OPERATION SAFEHOUSE. 193

OPERATION BLOWOUT 199

OPERATION BUGOUT. 205

OPERATION SKIDMARK. 211

INTRODUCTION

///

Missions Overview

Listen up cadets we won't waste your time with a bunch of rules but you need to get some things straight if you want to complete your missions and take part in the "Celebration of Man." What's that you say? Read on and you'll understand.

Missions to Manhood

Your C.O. will give you the mission guide which includes all information needed to complete your task. These missions will help you on your Journey to being a Man. Along the way, you will learn valuable skills like how to dig a foxhole. How to tie knots to stop an invading biker gang. In Operation Timbuktu you'll navigate your C.O. to a destination of your choice.

Read the mission guide once, think about what's required then reread. You'll earn Man Points by completing specific tasks, but watch out you might lose points by not following the directions or keeping your worksite and living quarters clean. All along the way you have the Journey to Men guarantee you'll have fun.

Operating Independently

It is your job to complete the mission. The mission is for you. If you find yourself always asking your C.O. "What should I do," you are missing the point. The mission guides provide

enough information and your C.O. will provide you enough equipment to complete your task.

Terminology

Commanding Officer: otherwise known as your Mom, Dad, Aunt, Uncle, Grandparent or other adult type person who's on your Missions to Manhood with you.

Cadet: that's you!

Deployment: the process of gathering up your equipment and moving it to a specified destination.

Egyptian Gas Ants: a rare and little known insect from Egypt that has the power to knock out small villages with its noxious gas fumes. Scientists are working on a serum to combat the gas' effects.

Fast Mover: a jet fighter or bomber.

H.Q. or Headquarters: your home, where you live. Inside H.Q. is your living quarters.

K.P. or Kitchen Patrol: doing dishes, cleaning up the kitchen area.

L.Z. or Landing Zone: the area where you will camp for the night, a meeting location or where your aircraft will land.

Living Quarters: an apartment, condo, house wherever you lay your head down at night. You might also know this location as your bedroom.

MacGyver: a fictional character from a 1980s TV show who famously could figure a way out of a tight spot using things around him, a Swiss army knife and duct tape. Do yourself a favor and watch some episodes online.

Squad: for the purposes of Journey to Men a squad is your direct family and anyone you live with at your H.Q.

The Celebration of Man

At the completion of your Missions to Manhood you will attend the Celebration of Man. This is a special event that will reward you for your hard work and focus on your tasks. We will not spoil the details of the celebration but be sure you have achieved enough Man Points to attend.

KNIFE GUIDE
HOW TO PROPERLY USE
AND CARE FOR A POCKET KNIFE

Cut Rope, Remove Bark, General Knifework

Saw Branches, Descale Fish, Cut PVC Pipe

Open Can of Beans, Philips Screwdriver

Cut Off Shirt Tags, Trim your Nails, Remove a Cast

Whittle, Fine Knife Work

Open Bottles, Strip Wires, Flathead Screwdriver

Remove Slivers, Pluck Eyebrows, Perform Surgery

Tighten Hockey Skates, Loosen Knots, Remove Fish Hooks

Open Mom's Wine, Remove Tire Valves, Attach Knife to Wall

Sew Leather or Tarps, Ream Holes, Chip Ice

My first knife was a Victorinox Swiss Army Explorer similar to the Huntsman but had a magnifying glass instead of a saw. The magnifying glass was not terribly useful other than to burn ants on a hot day (don't burn ants kids). I vividly remember that knife and wish I had it to this day. I've had many knives over the years, but none have impacted my self-esteem and sense of self like that red-coated beauty.

POCKET KNIFE SAFETY:

You can figure it out, it's a knife, it's sharp it cuts things, and it doesn't care what it is: wood, sausages, your thumb. When cutting always hold the knife with a firm grip and cut away from your body. If you are holding a piece of wood to sharpen it, make sure that your non-knife-holding hand is not in the blade's path. Be aware of a cutting activity that may cause the blade to fold over on your hand. I got a bad cut as a boy doing just that, treat your knife with the respect it deserves. With the Huntsman, the small blade is best for whittling because it will give you a lot more control and help keep your fingers safe.

CARING FOR YOUR POCKET KNIFE:

Victorinox crafts your knife out of stainless steel which means it won't rust easily, but you need to be sure and clean your blades after use. To perform correctly your knife should be clean at all times. You can use a wet paper towel or rag to clean it, or some simple green if you've got some tape residue on there. Just be sure to use a dry cloth at the end of your cleaning cycle to remove all moisture.

SHARPENING YOUR POCKET KNIFE:

Knives are safer when they are sharp and definitely more useful. Sharpening can be a tricky business, to get the best results you must sharpen your blades on a whetstone at approximately 20 degrees. Truthfully it's challenging to get it right, and you can easily make your knife duller. The Smith's Pocket Pal Sharpener is a great little inexpensive sharpener to keep your pocket knife at peak condition. You pull your knife through the correct groove 5 times to return your blade to optimum sharpness.

MAN POINTS FOR EVERYDAY CARRY:

During our 25 Missions to Manhood, your C.O. may perform spot checks to verify if you are carrying your knife. Have it on you at the right time and earn an extra 100 Man Points. Excellent.

OPERATION TIMBUKTU
NAVIGATE A MECHANIZED VEHICLE TO A FIXED WAYPOINT

MISSION BRIEFING:

Your mission is to navigate your C.O.'s (parental unit) vehicle to a location of your mutual choosing and the return trip to command H.Q. This location should be outside the scope of your regular daily travels such as a restaurant, army surplus store, break dancing academy or the like. Technology use is appropriate for the route planning portion of the assignment only.

EQUIPMENT:

Mission notebook, a pen or pencil, access to a computer or device for research on https://www.google.com/maps or similar mapping site.

MISSION DETAILS:

Once you have determined your waypoint, you must

determine your course from your command H.Q. (home). Your C.O. will not be providing any navigation information they will only pilot the vehicle based on your directions. Some things to consider and write down in your mission notebook:

» The address of the location.

» The address of your command H.Q.

» What are the names of streets, highways, and freeways you may need to travel on your journey?

» What are the turns and distance of each leg of your route?

» An overview map of your route.

» The ETD (estimated time to destination), remember to take into account traffic and other challenges.

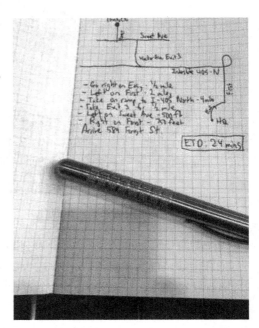

For researching your route, you might find https://google. com/maps helpful for planning your journey.

MISSION PARAMETERS:

You are the assigned navigator, and your C.O. is only participating as your driver. Brief your driver on the planned route and provide constant updates once your trip has begun. Constant feedback such as turn left in 2 miles on Easy Street

will be important. Giving the driver plenty of warning for an upcoming change is key to a successful trip. If you make a wrong turn or discover a problem with the route you will need to adjust the course and provide guidance to the driver.

Your only navigation tools available to you once the trip has begun will be your mission notebook.

MISSION VALUE:

»   +500 MAN POINTS FOR SUCCESSFULLY NAVIGATING TO THE WAYPOINT

»   +500 MAN POINTS FOR SUCCESSFULLY NAVIGATING TO H.Q.

»   +100 MAN POINTS FOR ARRIVING WITHIN 10 MINUTES OF ETD

»   -250 MAN POINTS FOR REQUIRING OUTSIDE HELP

OPERATION METAKNIFE
LEARN KNIFE SKILLS
AND WHITTLE A LETTER OPENER

MISSION BRIEFING:

Your mission is to familiarize yourself with your everyday carry tool and to use it to whittle a wood knife letter opener or similar project.

EQUIPMENT:

Pocket knife, wood from branches, mission notebook, sandpaper (optional).

MISSION DETAILS:

01. Familiarize yourself with your pocket knife and proper knife handling safety available in the Knife Guide.

02. Review the sample knife picture. Note that the handle still has the bark on it except for some additional rings for visual appearance. There is also a carved area of the handle that's perfect for personalizing with a name or date or saying.

03. Select the wood for your project. Good places to look are around your home, at your neighbors, at your grandparents or most anywhere there are trees. If it's not your property, be sure to ask permission before taking the wood, and it's best to use some fallen

branches about the thickness of your thumb or slightly bigger. You want a branch without a lot of moss or dirt on it. In some cases you may be able to prune some wood from a living tree using your Swiss Army saw blade.

WHITTLE A WOODEN KNIFE/ LETTER OPENER

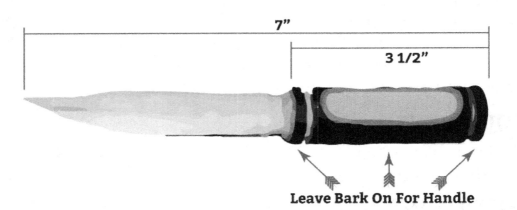

Leave Bark On For Handle

What types of wood are suitable for whittling? Most any are worth a shot, different parts of the country and world have different local trees so something like alders, maples, pines, apple, flowing plum, birch, oak and even some types of shrub material will work as well. It doesn't hurt to experiment, find a branch and give it a try.

04. Plan out your whittling project, it may make sense to sketch your design in your notebook ahead of time. You can draw in full size to get an idea if your knife looks right. There are no wrong answers here, let your imagination go. What are some other knives you've seen? Would they work for your carving project?

05.   Begin whittling your project. You can carve it in any order you want, this is your mission, you set the rules. The best blade for your carving work, if you are using a swiss army knife, is your small blade. It is plenty big for the job but lets you do more detail work without problems. Take your time, whittling should be an enjoyable way to pass the time and use your creative side.

06.   Finish your carving by sanding the blade and lightly sanding the handle. This is an optional step if you are happy with the rough look of your letter opener than perfect. Otherwise, you can start with some 120 grit sandpaper on the blade and then finish it off with a 220 grit sandpaper to make it very smooth.

07.   Clean up your work area and remove all chips

MISSION PARAMETERS:

Your primary mission is to get comfortable with the pocket knife that you should have on you at all times. Ok, not when you are showering, sleeping or at school but every other time.

MISSION VALUE:

»   +1000 MAN POINTS FOR A WELL WHITTLED LETTER OPENER

»   +100 MAN POINTS FOR A SPOT INSPECTION BY YOUR C.O. FINDING YOU CARRYING YOUR KNIFE

»   -250 MAN POINTS FOR LEAVING A MESSY WORK AREA

OPERATION GOOD NEIGHBOR
HELP A NEIGHBOR IN NEED

MISSION BRIEF:

This mission is simple but important. Being a good neighbor is not just a mission; it should be a way of life. If your neighbors can't count on those around them to help in a time of need, who can they rely on? It's known as the Golden

Rule and is one of the most important things you can learn. It's this: Love Your Neighbor as Yourself. What does that mean? It means you should treat others how you want to be treated and love them even when it might be difficult or not particularly enjoyable. You'll go find a neighbor (one you think might most need the help) and go offer your support and assistance. Now you will provide whatever help they need or figure out how to get it to them.

EQUIPMENT:

Whatever you need to help out.

MISSION DETAILS:

01. Pick your neighbor you will go help.

02. Tell your C.O. about your mission and where you are going.

03. Go talk to your neighbor being very polite and ask if there are jobs around the house that might need doing. If they say they don't need any help, maybe mention some skills you have and suggest some ideas. Some ideas that might be helpful: lawn care, weeding, picking up dog waste, house cleaning, sidewalk sweeping. If they still refuse your help leave them the option to ask you for help in the future and return home to brainstorm about something you could make them, cookies, a letter opener, birdhouse or something else.

04. Write down in your mission notebook how it felt to help out someone in need. Share your experience with your friends and family.

MISSION PARAMETERS:

This is your mission if you would like your C.O. to come with you when you go offer your help that is fine, but you need to be the one offering assistance. Your C.O. is just there to supervise.

/JTM/MISSIONOPS/GOODNEIGHBOR

MISSION VALUE:

» +1000 MAN POINTS HELPING YOUR
  NEIGHBOR

» +1000 MAN POINTS HELPING AN ADDITIONAL
  NEIGHBOR

OPERATION INFERNO
BUILD AND START A FIRE

MISSION BRIEF:

Creating fire is an essential skill for wilderness survival, cooking and roasting marshmallows. In this mission, we'll assemble the equipment and materials necessary to build a fire outdoors using Swedish firesteel and a great firestarter product created from cotton balls and Vaseline or petroleum jelly. As always, we'll do this safely.

EQUIPMENT:

Swedish firesteel or Ferro rod, cotton balls, and petroleum jelly. If you're searching for a brand of firesteel, the UCO Light My Fire Mini Swedish Firesteel is an excellent choice. It comes with a small scraper to create the spark. This is superior to using a pocket knife for obvious safety reasons. It is readily available in sporting and outdoor stores and online.

MISSION DETAILS:

Gather your materials and find some suitable firewood. Your cotton balls soaked with Vaseline will make excellent tinder, and you will just need to build a teepee with gradually increasing thickness of dry wood which we'll cover in more detail below.

01. PRACTICE USING YOUR FIRESTEEL

Firesteel is a little trickier to use than a match or lighter but is a great item to carry with you hiking or when out in the woods as it doesn't matter if it gets wet and will last for thousands of lights. If you have the Swedish Firesteel, we recommend it has a stainless steel striker to make the spark.

IMPORTANT: when new your firesteel comes with a protective coating that will wear away as you drag your striker down the rod and the spark will get bigger as it wears away. The striker has a directional arrow stamped on the handle. You'll notice it works significantly better in the proper position.

Give it a try generating some sparks in a safe area by dragging the striker down the rod. You don't have to push hard nor do you have to strike the firesteel. Just scrape it down the rod rather quickly and you should be giving off some large sparks in no time. You can also use your knife in a pinch although the striker included will work best and is much safer.

02. MAKE SOME COTTON BALL FIRESTARTERS

This is a messy assignment so be sure to clean your work area as well as your hands. In a Ziploc back add a dab of Vaseline and three cotton balls. Work the cotton balls in the bag to coat with Vaseline. You can even do this without ever putting your fingers in the bag to keep the mess away. Make a few cotton ball firestarters to save for later and just keep them in the bag.

03. PREPARE YOUR SITE FOR A FIRE

Make sure you have a C.O. approved area for building a fire,

either an existing fire pit or an area you cleared out away from other flammable items. Get permission before proceeding.

04. BUILD YOUR TEPEE

There are many ways to build a fire, for this mission we are going to focus on building the Tepee. It is a very efficient fire to get going and works well even with wet wood. Gather some sticks or other dry kindling and stack it in a cone over your cotton firestarter tinder. Make sure there are some small thin branches and then add a few larger pieces of wood on the

outside of your tepee. Once your fire is lit, the pieces of wood will burn down and start to fall in feeding the fire.

05. LIGHT THE FIRE

Place your cotton balls at the center of your tepee or cone. Make sure you are upwind to keep the wind from putting out the start of your fire. Get close to your cotton balls and direct a spark or two from your firesteel towards the firestarter. With a bit of practice, they should start right up.

06. FEED THE FIRE

Make sure you have more wood for the fire staged nearby and that it is relatively dry. As the fire starts to take you can slowly add additional wood.

07. MAKE SOME S'MORES!

08. DOUSE THE FIRE

When you finish with your fire, you need to make sure you completely extinguish the flames. Douse the fire with water and then spread out the coals and douse a little more. Keep an eye on it for 10 minutes or so to be sure it doesn't rekindle itself.

MISSION PARAMETERS:

Building a fire is good fun and a very practical skill for any cadet. Be sure it's safe and legal to burn in your area before you begin this mission. Safety is important, your C.O. should supervise this entire process.

MISSION VALUE:

» +250 MAN POINTS FOR SUCCESSFULLY USING YOUR FIRESTEEL

» +250 MAN POINTS FOR MAKING AND LIGHTING YOUR COTTON BALLS

» +500 MAN POINTS FOR BUILDING A FIRE LASTING LONGER THAN 10 MINUTES

» -1000 MAN POINTS FOR NOT DOUSING YOUR FIRE

OPERATION PACKMULE
READY YOUR GEAR FOR TRAVEL AND LOAD VEHICLE

MISSION BRIEF:

When preparing for a trip or adventure outfitting yourself with the proper equipment is critical. In this mission, you will prepare for an upcoming trip or vacation by gathering your gear. Further, if this trip requires vehicle travel, you'll help assemble the rest of the squad's gear and pack it efficiently and effectively.

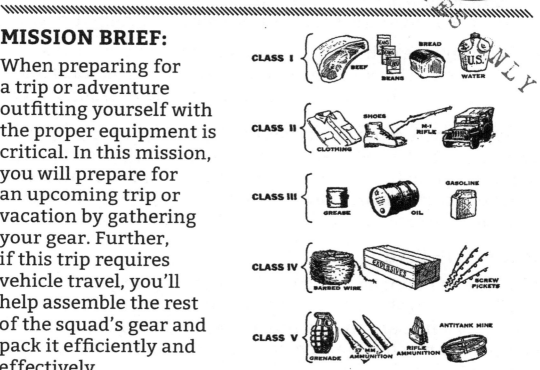

EQUIPMENT:

Bag or suitcase for stowing your gear (this should never be a garbage bag). Gear to go in your bag. Suggested packing list from mission guide.

MISSION DETAILS:

Before you get to packing your bag, you need to gather some intel from your travel advisor or C.O. Answering the following questions will help determine your equipment needs.

» Where are we going? Research the
weather for your trip, is it raining,
snowing, desert hot?

» How long will we be traveling? A longer
duration adventure will require more clothing items.

» Why are we going? Is this for a formal affair? Is it a
vacation? This will help determine if you need to bring
your dress uniform, bathing suit, sunglasses, sunscreen.

Now you know more about your trip you'll need to gather
your gear. Make your bed and that will be the perfect place
to lay out your equipment and clothing. While not perfect
for every trip, the included mission packing checklist will
provide an excellent starting point for your task.

PACK THE CAR

If your trip happens to involve a road trip of any sort (lucky
you!) then you should help out and pack the car. Packing
the car is a fine art and a valuable skill that only few can
completely master, we have faith in you cadet! The most
important part is to gather all of your luggage, dogs, sports
equipment, tents, firewood, and whatever else you are going
to bring first and set it next to your rig.

01. Now think about who's coming on this trip and where
will they sit, so you know what space you have available.

02. If the family pet is coming along where are they going
to ride? Keep that in mind as you pack.

03. Are there items you are going to want access to easily as
you're traveling like a cooler? Make sure you take that
into account when stowing your gear.

PACKING LIST

CLOTHING
- [ ] Shoes (running or dress)
- [ ] Sandals or Flip Flops
- [ ] Socks (# per days traveling)
- [ ] Pants (2+)
- [ ] Shorts (2+)
- [ ] UNDERWEAR!!!!! At least 2 pair (# per days traveling)
- [ ] T-Shirts (2+)
- [ ] Dress Shirts
- [ ] Hat
- [ ] Sweatshirt
- [ ] Coat
- [ ] Swimsuit
- [ ] Belt
- [ ] Sunglasses
- [ ] Extra Glasses

TOILETRIES
- [ ] Toothbrush
- [ ] Toothpaste
- [ ] Soap
- [ ] Shampoo
- [ ] Wash cloth
- [ ] Deodorant
- [ ] Plastic Ziploc bag for Toiletries
- [ ] Comb or Brush

MEDICAL
- [ ] Required Medication
- [ ] Sunscreen
- [ ] Allergy medication

SPORT
- [ ] Swim Goggles
- [ ] Raft
- [ ] Floaties
- [ ] Inflatable Alligator
- [ ] Frisbee
- [ ] Ball (Football, Basketball)
- [ ] Kite
- [ ] Scooter / Bike

READY GEAR
- [ ] Passport or ID if necessary
- [ ] Pocket Knife (not on plane)
- [ ] Notebook
- [ ] Pen
- [ ] Firestarter (camping, etc.)
- [ ] Duct Tape
- [ ] Flash light

SLEEPING
- [ ] Sleeping Bag
- [ ] Sleep Sack or Sheet
- [ ] Pillow
- [ ] Mattress Pad

RECREATION
- [ ] Money
- [ ] Reading Material
- [ ] Music Player
- [ ] Phone
- [ ] Charging cables
- [ ] Camera

04. Put in the heavy durable items first. Meaning stuff that won't get smashed. Think about their sizes and maximize space.

05. You can now add softer unbreakable items to the car and shove into holes in your load. Pillows, sleeping bags, and clothes in a duffel bag are good options.

06. Fragile breakable items go last. Often you can use some softer gear to make sure Mom's glass figurines are secure.

07. Is it just not working? Don't be afraid to pull the load out and start over.

08. Don't forget your squad's luggage!

MISSION PARAMETERS:

You are responsible for your own gear. You might be unhappy arriving at your sweet water slide adventure only to realize you didn't bring any swim trunks, but you won't do that again. So pay attention to the details, review the packing list and you'll be ready for your trip while providing a valuable service to your squad.

MISSION VALUE:

» +1000 MAN POINTS FOR PACKING YOUR GEAR

» +500 MAN POINTS FOR PACKING THE CAR

OPERATION PENNYPINCH
SAVING FOR A BIG TICKET ITEM

MISSION BRIEF:

In this mission you'll identify a big-ticket item (maybe in the $100-200 range), make a savings plan and track your progress to your goal. Working with your commanding officer (C.O.) you might also explore opening a bank account.

EQUIPMENT:

Savings goal sheet (download at https://journeytomen.com/downloads), mission notebook.

MISSION DETAILS:

01. This is the fun part. Do some dreaming and come up with an item you want to purchase. Some examples from previous squad missions include an Airsoft machine gun, a PA system for their band, wireless

headphones. Your goal should require saving money and will not include monies already on your person. Consider a savings goal that you can reach in a month or two with some hard work. Operation Pennypinch is part of your 25 missions, setting a goal you can achieve before all the tasks are complete will earn you an extra 1000 Man Points.

02.   Find a new page in your mission notebook and at the top put the item you are saving for and the cost. You should also put the same information in the savings sheet at the end of this mission document. Be sure you include sales tax in your cost if required where you live. Your C.O. might need to give you some guidance on the tax.

03.   Using your mission notebook write your ETA (estimated time of arrival) to hit your goal. If you think you could do it in 5 weeks, your ETA is 5 weeks.

04.   Now you have your total savings amount and the time to reach that goal work backward to determine how much money you have to save per day. How would you go about figuring that out? Write that out in your notebook doing the math.

05.   Keep track of your money on the savings sheet as part of this mission. Your first line should be the amount of money you have this would be your starting balance. If you earn money, you'd record that as a deposit (+) and you add that amount to your balance. If you buy something with your money that would be a withdrawal

(-) so you would subtract that from your current balance. You've reached your goal when your balance is equal to or greater than your goal cost. A filled out example is below.

SAVING FOR: Airsoft Gun   COST: $175.20

Date	Description	Withdrawal Amount (-)	Deposit Amount (+)	Balance
6/15	Starting Balance		+25.00	$25.00
6/18	Mowed Lawn		+15.00	$40.00
6/19	Bought Dad a Slurpee	-6.25		$33.75

06.   This would be a great time to open a bank account with your parental units. You'll learn about working with money, keeping track of your spending and earnings. Most bank accounts will require you have at least $25 to open the account and they might even give you a special prize for signing up.

07.   Now it's time to rise and grind and put your best effort into earning some money. Future mission Operation Kickstart will give you some ideas on how to do that but work with your C.O.'s for a list of things you can do around the house to save. Better yet, come up with a list of things you'll do for them beyond your normal chores to contribute to the household and earn some money.

MISSION VALUE:

» +500 MAN POINTS FOR SETTING A SAVINGS GOAL

» +250 MAN POINTS FOR FIGURING YOUR DAILY SAVINGS GOAL

» +1000 MAN POINTS FOR HITTING YOUR SAVINGS GOAL

SAVING FOR: **COST:**

Date	Description	Withdrawal Amount (-)	Deposit Amount (+)	Balance

OPERATION RISE AND SHINE
PREPARE BREAKFAST FOR YOUR SQUAD

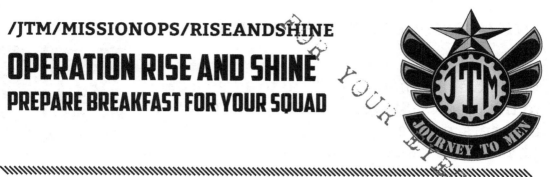

MISSION BRIEF:

Preparing a meal for yourself and others is a vital skill for any cadet. Breakfast is a great place to start your cooking adventure as you can experiment with various foods and recipes as your skills develop. Your mission is to feed your squad breakfast and includes: planning a breakfast menu, shopping for ingredients, cooking the meal and cleaning.

EQUIPMENT:

Ingredients for your meal such as eggs, bread, cereal, juice, pans and cooking implements, a kitchen.

MISSION DETAILS:

With your impending tactical breakfast engagement approaching, you must detail your meal plan. Detailed communication with your C.O. on the proper use of your kitchen equipment is critical to avoid a call to the medics. Stoves, toasters, microwaves, blenders, coffee makers all can cause you physical harm. Perform a walk through with your C.O. on the kitchen equipment you need to use and have them sign off before you begin. There are plenty of breakfast options available that don't require the use of dangerous kitchen equipment for the younger cadet. Shredded Wheat and orange juice are perfectly acceptable breakfast options. It is vital you ask for permission and supervision to ensure your safety while avoiding burning down command H.Q.

01. PLAN YOUR BREAKFAST MENU

Your first order of business is deciding what you will make for breakfast. Think about your guest's food preferences and what ingredients are in the pantry. Consider how much of each food item you must have on hand to make your recipes. Here are the general guidelines you can use for an adult, note this is just for each food item; this is not a suggested meal.

» 2 eggs

» 3 pieces of bacon

» 2 slices of toast

» 3 pancakes (standard size)

» 2 pieces of French toast

» 1 bowl of cereal or oatmeal

» 2 cups of coffee (plan on a refill for their original cup)

02.   MAKE A MENU

You need to inform your diners what they'll
be eating so you'll prepare a menu for them
to know their food choices. Make it easy on
yourself and provide a small set of options, for instance,
you'll provide one main meal course, and they can choose
what to drink.

03.   WRITE YOUR SHOPPING LIST

To prepare for your shopping trip, you must research what
ingredients are available at home. Note items you must
purchase in your mission notebook. Work with your C.O. to
acquire all the groceries.

04.   PREPARE YOUR WORK AREA

Make sure your cooking area is clean, and you have all the
food and kitchen implements at hand. It's best to do this
before you cook as breakfast foods finish quickly. Clean off
the counters and your dining table. Put out plates, knives,
spoons, forks, glasses. Set the table so you can eat right away
once your food is prepared. Setting the table is an excellent
job for the more junior members of your squad if they are on
site.

05.   COOK BREAKFAST

You are primarily on your own for figuring out the cooking
process. Above all else be safe and if any part of the cooking
process concerns you ask for your C.O.'s guidance. If you are
preparing something like pancakes and eggs, you'll often
have to prepare the pancakes in batches. Setting the oven on
low (175 degrees) and putting the pancakes on an oven-safe
plate will keep those pancakes nice and hot. This works for

French toast as well.

Think about the order of preparation. If you are making coffee, that should happen first. If any of the ingredients require preparation like peeling, cutting, slicing tackle that next. If you are making pancakes or waffles mix up the batter. Whisk scrambled eggs ahead of time and set aside you will cook those last. Any cooked items should be nice and hot when you serve them to your squad.

06. CLEAN UP

Your C.O. will be much more likely to allow your cooking exploits to continue if you do a thorough job cleaning up after yourself. Everything back where it came from, dishes, pots and pans clean. Be sure to wipe any tables and counters.

MISSION PARAMETERS:

This is a perfect team mission. If you have brothers or sisters living at H.Q., enlist their help on this task. Above all else be safe.

MISSION POINTS:

» +1000 MAN POINTS FOR DELIVERING BREAKFAST

» +500 MAN POINTS FOR A SPOTLESS KITCHEN AFTERWARDS

» -500 MAN POINTS FOR NOT CLEANING UP AFTER YOURSELF

OPERATION BROKENSPOKE
OVERHAUL AND MAINTAIN YOUR BICYCLE

MISSION BRIEF:

Your mission is to clean, lubricate, inspect and optionally repair your two-wheeler. Keeping your vehicles in good working order is vital to field exercises, running to the store or escaping a roving biker gang.

EQUIPMENT:

Bicycle or another vehicle, hose, bucket, car wash soap, sponge or wash mitt, towel, Simple Green cleaner or similar, brush (tooth or other), rag, lubricant, bike multi-tool, wrenches.

MISSION DETAILS:

01.   READY YOUR WASHING STATION

First, prepare your work area and gather your mission

equipment. The driveway, side alley or most anywhere you can get away with spraying a hose will work. Fill your bucket up about 3/4 full of water (about a gallon or two of water) and add a quick pour of carwash or other liquid soap. Adding the soap and spraying in more water will cause it to foam up nicely.

02.   WASH YOUR BIKE

Give your vehicle a good spray down with the hose. Now get out your wash mitt, dip it in the bucket and clean your bike. Stay away from the chain and sprockets at this point with your cleaning mitt to keep it from getting greasy, you'll handle that next. Get all the nooks and crannies like under your seat and forks. Once you've finished soaping give it a good rinse and then dry it off with your towel.

03.   DEGREASE YOUR CHAIN AND SPROCKETS

Your chain is your driveline to freedom. If it's rusty or damaged, you might quickly find yourself stranded. Keeping the driveline clean and lubricated is a simple step to ensure the proper operation of your vehicle. Spray the chain and sprockets with Simple Green or similar degreaser and use your brush to scrub the cleaner on all parts of your chain.

An excellent way to work on your bike at this point is to turn your bike upside down so it's resting on its handlebars and seat. You can turn your pedals by hand and move the chain along to be sure you have cleaned all parts. Also, be sure you degrease your sprockets, front and back. Finish by using your rag to wipe the components dry.

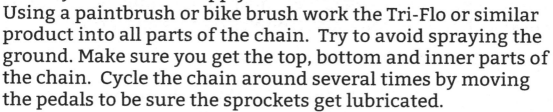

04. LUBRICATE YOUR CHAIN AND SPROCKETS

Now that the chain and sprockets are clean and dry it's crucial to apply a lubricant.
Using a paintbrush or bike brush work the Tri-Flo or similar product into all parts of the chain. Try to avoid spraying the ground. Make sure you get the top, bottom and inner parts of the chain. Cycle the chain around several times by moving the pedals to be sure the sprockets get lubricated.

05. TIGHTEN LOOSE BOLTS, GENERAL SAFETY CHECK

Now that your rig is clean and lubed, it's time to check the critical equipment. Check any nut, screw or bolt on it and make sure it's tight. This is the time to use your adjustable wrench or your bike multi-tool. If your chain is loose and comes off frequently, you can loosen the two nuts on either side of your rear wheel and slide the whole mechanism back to tighten. If you tighten the hub too much, your wheel might have issues rolling. When you re-tighten the nuts be sure that the wheel sits straight between the frame, give it a spin to be sure.

06. BRAKE CHECK

Proper operation of your brakes is a critical safety step. You need to be sure you can stop when you need to, as you know Mom really hates it when she has to take you to the emergency room. If you have a coaster brake (push back on the pedals to stop), they should just work. If they don't you need some professional help, talk to your C.O. If you have hand brakes check their operation, do they squeeze too far? There is an adjusting nut on the cables you can unscrew to tighten the tension. Check your brake pads are they worn down, if so you must get some new ones, sounds like Operation Timbuktu again.

07. TAKE A TEST RIDE

If your bike operates well, your mission is complete, excellent work! Otherwise, you must troubleshoot its operation.

08. CLEAN UP YOUR WORK AREA

A vital step to avoid K.P. duty or push-ups is the proper clean-up of your work area. Finally, return all of your tools and supplies to their appropriate locations.

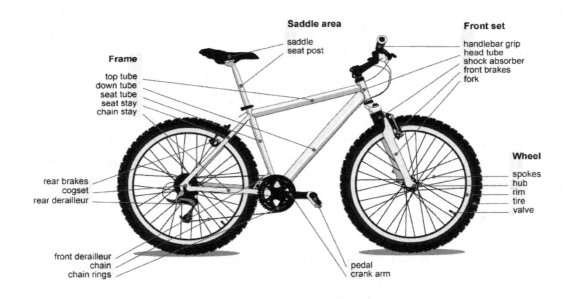

MISSION PARAMETERS:

This mission is yours to complete. Perform all mission steps and if you have issues with your bike operation or need additional repairs, then and only then can you talk to your C.O. with your plan.

MISSION VALUE:

- » +500 MAN POINTS FOR A CLEAN VEHICLE
- » +500 MAN POINTS FOR LUBRICATING AND TIGHTENING ALL BOLTS
- » +250 MAN POINTS FOR FULLY FUNCTIONING BRAKES
- » -250 MAN POINTS FOR A DIRTY WORK AREA

OPERATION GAS PUMPER
FUEL THE SQUAD TRANSPORT

MISSION BRIEF:

Keeping your vehicle operational and ready to roll is a critical component of your journey to being men. In this mission, you'll fuel your squad's car and do a spot safety check to make sure your rig is safe for the road.

EQUIPMENT:

A vehicle, you're C.O.'s payment source.

MISSION DETAILS:

Your C.O. will maneuver your vehicle within reach of a gas fueling pump. What payment type will you be using to purchase the fuel? Determine what kind of gasoline your vehicle requires. Your choices are usually: diesel, unleaded (regular), unleaded (mid-grade), unleaded (premium). If you look inside the fuel filler door on the car, it will typically provide information on the recommended gas type.

Never put diesel fuel in a regular gas vehicle. The nozzle sizes are different between regular gas and diesel, and it should be nearly impossible to insert into the gas filler tube. Confirm the correct fuel type before you perform the next steps. In the same vein never put regular unleaded gasoline into a diesel fuel tank. You can cause permanent damage to the vehicle by using the wrong fuel type.

01. If you are using a debit or credit card for payment, you'll need more information for the transaction to occur. For a credit card, you must know the billing Zip code, and for a debit card, you must know the PIN code. Follow the prompts on the gas pump to provide your payment information. If you are paying cash head on into the station and pre-pay, make a note of the # located at the top of the pump. You must pick which type of gas you will use which is usually a button labeled with the gas type.

02. Open up your gas door on your car or truck and remove the gas cap. Twist it counter-clockwise (to the left) to remove. Usually, there is a slot on the gas door where you can set the gas cap to keep it out of the way.

03. Remove the gas nozzle from the pump, and sometimes, you must flip up the lever that the nozzle was resting on to activate the pump. Use the end of the gas nozzle to do that so you don't get gas on your hands. Put the nozzle firmly into the gas tank filler tube of the vehicle.

04. Squeeze the handle of the gas pump fully to start the

gas pumping. On most nozzles, there is a tab or hook you can engage to keep the pump running without having to hold the handle down.

05. The gas pump will stop automatically when the tank is full or if you've hit your limit of money prepaid. Wait about 3 seconds then carefully remove the nozzle being careful not to drip any gas on yourself and put it back in the gas pump.

06. Put the gas cap back on your tank. It is essential you turn it all the way to the right clockwise until you hear about 3 clicks to be sure it's sealed.

07. Now do a quick walk around tires. They should have enough pressure so they don't look like they are flattening out, see the example picture. If the tire is low, then pull over to the tire inflation station and add some air.

08. Do a general check on the lights noting any damage or cracks. You can also have your C.O. do a light test while you verify the brake lights, turn signals, and headlights are all working.

09. You're all done! Now your C.O. should never have to pump their own gas ever again!

/JTM/MISSIONOPS/GASPUMPER

MISSION PARAMETERS:

Be safe when pumping gas, touch the side of your vehicle when getting out. This will ground you keeping any form of static electricity from setting off the gasoline vapors. Try not to get gas on your hands, it takes a lot of scrubbing to get the smell off.

MISSION VALUE:

» +1000 MAN POINTS FOR SUCCESSFULLY FUELING THE FAMILY VEHICLE

OPERATION KICKSTART
START A KID SMALL BUSINESS

MISSION BRIEF:

In Operation Pennypinch you set a savings target, now in Operation Kickstart, you'll start a small business to earn money towards your goal. A kid business should be simple, use one of our ideas or come up with your own and you'll be bringing in money in no time.

EQUIPMENT:

Mission Notebook, whatever materials your business may require.

MISSION DETAILS:
01. DEVELOP A BUSINESS PLAN

Brainstorm some ideas for your business.
You could try offering a service like the ones listed on the
ideas page. You could sell some of your stuff at a garage sale
or with your C.O.'s permission on eBay or Craigslist. How
about building or creating something to sell? Could you sell
the letter openers you whittled in Operation Metaknife? If
you like to cook or bake, you could whip up some cookies or
treats for the neighborhood.

02. NAME YOUR BUSINESS

Any small business has a name, and yours should be no
different. Maybe a name related to what you are offering
like Billy's Carwashorama.

03. DETERMINE WHAT TO CHARGE CUSTOMERS

Take some time to determine how much to charge for your
services or set a price for items you are selling. If you take
time to build something you should charge at least what it
takes to make your item including materials and your time.
The national minimum wage that workers earn in 2019 is
$7.25 an hour that's a beginning point. For instance, if you
can make 4 letter openers in 3 hours at $7.25 an hour it costs
you 3 * 7.25 / 4 or $5.44 per letter opener. For this item $6-10
is a fair price.

You should have a price sheet ready to go for your customers
because that will be one of the first things they will want to
know. Write this down in your mission notebook.

04. DEVELOP YOUR PITCH

A pitch is what you call telling your customers about your business. Here's one for dog poop removal: "Hello Neighbor, are you tired of picking up after Fluffy after he does his business? For only $10 a week Poopmasters will come by and remove all of your doody for you, leaving your weekend free for relaxing." Write one down in your mission notebook for your own business. It shouldn't be too long, something you could rehearse and say in about 30 seconds maximum.

05. WHO ARE YOUR CUSTOMERS?

You need to know who you are selling your products to; we call this market research. Is it your neighbors, your grandparents, people at your C.O.'s office, commuters driving by your house? Don't forget your parents as a potential customer.

06. GO SELL IT!

Go pound the pavement and find some customers. Do not despair if the first potential customer turns you down, keep trying.

MISSION PARAMETERS:

Be Safe! Make sure your C.O. knows all about your business and how are you going to do it and where.

You may not make thousands of dollars with your business idea but doing something you create yourself is a lot of fun and rewarding. Develop your own thoughts and run them by your C.O. for their guidance. You might even want to pitch your service to them and see if they'll be your first customer.

Above all else make sure you know exactly what you are providing and how much it costs.

A WORD ABOUT PROFIT

Profit is the amount of money you make after you subtract all of your costs to provide that service or product. If you're selling ice cream and it costs $.50 an ice cream bar, and you sell them at $1.25 a piece that's $.75 profit on each bar sold. Make sure you take into account your costs to provide your service or product as that will definitely impact your bottom line.

MISSION VALUE:

» +250 MAN POINTS FOR WRITING A BUSINESS PLAN: SERVICE, COMPANY NAME, PRICE SHEET AND PITCH

» +1000 MAN POINTS FOR MAKING A PROFIT OF $10 IN A DAY

» +5000 MAN POINTS FOR MAKING A PROFIT OF $50 IN A DAY

» -250 MAN POINTS FOR LEAVING A MESSY WORK AREA

SMALL BUSINESS IDEAS

SERVICES

- ❑ Dog Poop Removal
- ❑ Dog Walking
- ❑ Dog Washing
- ❑ Mow Lawns
- ❑ Weed Gardens
- ❑ Wash Cars
- ❑ Wash Boats
- ❑ Wash RV's
- ❑ Clean and setup Garage Sales
- ❑ Window Washing
- ❑ Pressure Washing
- ❑ Babysitting

BUILD THINGS TO SELL

- ❑ Letter Opener, Carved Items
- ❑ Bird Houses
- ❑ Survival Bracelets
- ❑ Picnic Table
- ❑ Planter Boxes

SELL FOOD ITEMS

- ❑ Sell Ice Cream/Popsicles
- ❑ Cookies
- ❑ Powerade/Gatorade to cyclists
- ❑ Pizza
- ❑ Donuts to morning commuters

OPERATION CONDOR
BUILD A BIRDHOUSE

MISSION BRIEF:

Your mission is to build a birdhouse. This birdhouse should not be for a condor as a condor is actually the largest flying bird in North America also known as a vulture. Operation Condor just sounds cooler than Operation Tufted Titmouse. A birdhouse is a classic woodworking project and a great place to start. This house will provide an excellent place for your winged friends to live and also makes a great item to sell for Operation Kickstart.

EQUIPMENT:

Mission notebook, cedar fence

boards 1x4x6 and 1x6x6 or similar, miter box, saw, drill, 1 1/2" drill bit, hammer, 6D Galvanized nails, tape measure, pencil, and square. Perch material like a branch, golf tee or dowel, safety glasses.

MISSION DETAILS:

01.   DESIGN THE BIRDHOUSE

Throughout this document are example birdhouses you could model for your own design. Using your mission notebook draw out your plan complete with measurements. If you have a graph paper notebook one square is 1/4" but to make it so you can draw a scaled-down version you can say that each square in real life is 1/2" so if you were to draw a 6x8" birdhouse it would measure only 3x4" or 12 squares by 16 squares.

Think about the roof design. We have a neat birdhouse made with a car license plate as a roof, where could you get your hands on some old plates? Or you could just use the cedar fence boards for the top. Make several drawings showing the sides and then the front to give you different views. Take into account where the opening for the birdhouse belongs on your plan along with a suitable location for the perch that mounts to the outside of your house.

Different size birds need different size holes for their entrance, a good size for a variety of birds is 1 1/2" in diameter.

02. LAYOUT AND CUT

Gather your materials and tools. Before you cut up your lumber think about laying out your cuts so you can make the best use of your wood. Now using your tape measure, a pencil and a square or ruler mark your first cut and saw the board. If you have access to a miter box, it is a useful tool for cutting nice straight lines. Otherwise take your time, sawing by hand is great exercise. You must cut your 2 sides, the front, back, bottom, and the roof. Do a test fit of all your pieces and re-saw as necessary.

03. DRILL THE OPENING

It's probably easiest at this point to drill the opening for the birdhouse. Mark a center point and use that for your drilling location. If you have questions regarding drilling or the safety of drilling, please talk to your C.O.

04. ASSEMBLE THE BIRDHOUSE

Measure and mark the locations for your nails for a nice orderly look or just nail, it's up to you. Try to keep

your nail locations at least a half inch from the edge of a board to minimize splitting of the wood.

05.   ATTACH THE PERCH

The perch is what the bird stands on before entering the birdhouse. It should be about an inch below the hole to allow the bird to enter. You can use a branch, a golf tee, even a screw. Drill a small hole for the branch to go in, a touch of glue will make it permanent.

MISSION PARAMETERS:

Be Safe! Tools are dangerous when used incorrectly. For all woodworking eye protection is a must, a stray piece of sawdust in your eye can be very unpleasant. Above all, use your imagination and have fun!

MISSION VALUE:

» +1000 MAN POINTS FOR A COMPLETED BIRDHOUSE

» +1000 MAN POINTS FOR EVIDENCE OF A BIRD USING YOUR HOUSE

» -250 MAN POINTS FOR LEAVING A MESSY WORK AREA

OPERATION CLEANSWEEP
READY AND CLEAN
YOUR LIVING QUARTERS

MISSION BRIEF:

As a cadet that's part of a larger family squad, it's your duty to clean up after yourself, simple as that. Your mission is to clean your primary living areas such as your bedroom, TV room, kitchen, bathroom or wherever you spend time. This might be a massive job if you rarely clean up, or a small one if you are better about not leaving your things about.

EQUIPMENT:

Household cleaning equipment, vacuum, broom, dusting materials, bathroom cleaners, garbage bag.

MISSION DETAILS:

You'll handle your individual rooms or areas using a combined 3 Wave Assault. Wave 1: Quick Tidy, Pickup, Wave 2: Cleaning, Wave 3: Final Mission round up and Vacuum

01.   START WITH YOUR ROOM

Your mission begins in your own living quarters to show your C.O. your appreciation for shelter and a warm bunk.

Wave 1: Full out assault on clutter and garbage.

Get a garbage sack and do a sweep removing all garbage and items that don't belong in your room. Go clockwise so you can focus on all areas of your space. Now using that same method pick up and tidy anything that's out of place in your room. Put it where it belongs, not in a corner, if you don't have a place for it, find one, or consider donating or recycling.

Tidying means to arrange things so they look nice and orderly. If you have a book you want to leave out on your desk arrange it so it's in line with the edges of your desktop.

If you have dirty laundry put it in the laundry basket or in a pile, you'll handle in Wave 2. If you have clean clothes lying around put them on your bed you'll handle in that next Wave. This is not the time to make 85 trips around the house putting things back. Items that don't belong in your room like your brother's Bag O'Vipers or your Dad's prized hammer place outside your door and handle in Wave 2.

Wave 2: Clean like the wind.

Using the same method as Wave 1 go clockwise in the same spot and work your way around dusting from the top of the wall to the bottom, getting everything as you go. Work from the top first as dust falls down as you go. Work quickly but thoroughly around the room. Now get your cleaners like Simple Green and a cloth and spray and wipe in an S fashion down all walls and surfaces focusing on fingerprints and gunk. Scan every inch of your room looking up and down as you go. Use window cleaner and clean your windows or mirrors in the same way.

Now put away that clean laundry you piled on your bed from before.

02.   MAKE YOUR BED.

Wave 3: Final jobs and finishing touches

Vacuum or sweep/mop your area. Again working clockwise get every inch of your floor, taking a little more time to be sure you get everything as clean as it should be. There should be nothing on the floor to block your way if you performed Wave 1 correctly. Move furniture around so you can vacuum under it. Yes, vacuum your closet too!

Take dirty laundry to its location such as a laundry room. Return any other items not belonging to your room to their location. Don't make the extra items somebody else's problem, put them away too.

03.   PREPARE FOR INSPECTION

Before moving on have your C.O. inspect your work for a job well done.

04.   MOVE ON TO THE NEXT ROOM

Talk with your C.O. about which room you should focus on next.

MISSION PARAMETERS:

Keeping your headquarters clean is a chore all members of the squad should share as they are able. Your C.O.'s provide you a place to live and you can show sincere appreciation and gratitude by performing these duties. Your bedroom is a base requirement but also clean any other room you use regularly or wherever your C.O. wants you to focus your resources.

MISSION VALUE:

» +1000 MAN POINTS FOR A CLEAN ROOM

» +500 MAN POINTS FOR EACH EXTRA AREA YOU CLEAN

» -1000 MAN POINTS FOR WHINING OR COMPLAINING

» -50 MAN POINTS FOR EACH ITEM NOT PICKED UP OR TRASH LAYING ABOUT

» -250 MAN POINTS FOR NOT MAKING YOUR BED

OPERATION KNOT MY JOB
KNOT TYING IN THE HEAT OF BATTLE

MISSION BRIEF:

Tying knots is a skill that is often overlooked, but as you'll see in this mission, it just might save your life!

EQUIPMENT:

Paracord or similar rope approximately 20 feet, a tree branch or pipe, tarp.

MISSION DETAILS:

This mission will focus on four knots to tie and when to use them. Knot tying

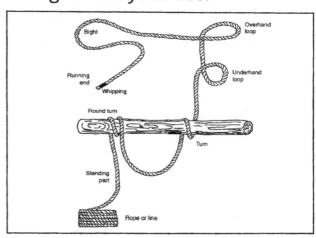

requires practice so that when your hovercraft landing vehicle is coming into port, you aren't watching Metube videos to figure out how to keep it from breaking free and destroying the dock. Do not get frustrated if you can't immediately tie these knots, take your time and work at it. For additional resources to help you learn we highly recommend a great App available for Apple and Android devices called Animated Knots by Grog it is well worth the money, or you can get access for free on their website https://www.animatedknots.com/.

01.   LEARN TO TIE THE BOWLINE KNOT

The bowline knot is a very useful knot for making a loop

that is very strong, of any length which is easy to untie. It's often used for securing loads, lifting or lowering loads and is useful in boating.

First, form a small loop while leaving a fair amount of rope for the size loop you want to make at the end. Take the end of the rope and run that through your small loop and behind

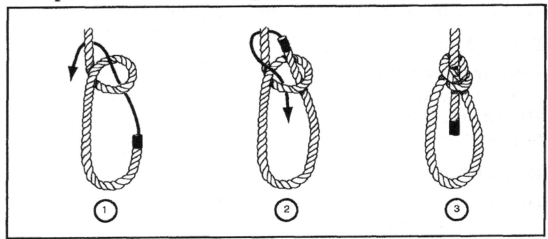

the standing part. Pull the rope again through the small loop and tighten. Work on tying this with different size loops so you can do it efficiently and quickly.

02.   LEARN TO TIE THE BUNTLINE HITCH

The buntline hitch is a good knot to use when you need to attach a rope to a log or a ring. As a bonus if you know this knot then you've conquered tying a neck tie known as the four in hand style.

Take the running end of your rope and pass it around your log and loop around the standing part. Pass it through the hole beside the log. Finally, make a half hitch to complete the knot. The illustration should help clarify the process.

03.   LEARN TO TIE A BUTTERFLY LOOP

We also know the butterfly loop as the lineman's loop or alpine butterfly loop. This

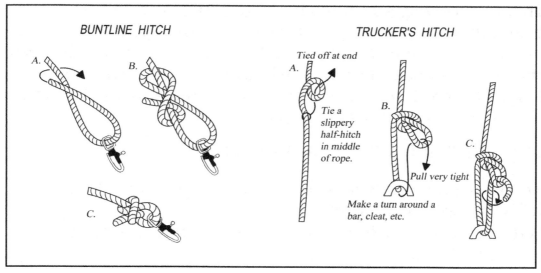

knot is useful for tying yourself off if you are mountaineering or combined with the Trucker's Hitch can tighten a load in the middle of a rope.

Make two twists in the same direction to form the two loops. Once you've done that you'll take the outer loop and put it

around the standing part and pull it through the inner loop hole.

04.   LEARN TO TIE A TRUCKER'S HITCH

This is relatively simple to tie once you've mastered a butterfly loop. Tie a butterfly loop leaving approximately 3 or 4 feet of remaining line. Pull the remaining line through the eye or hook and then loop back through the butterfly loop. Pull hard downward on the running end and then tie one or two half hitches to secure.

05.   PRACTICE, PRACTICE, PRACTICE

Keep working on these knots so you can perform them without looking at your mission guide or any other resource. When you feel confident, you are ready to move on to the Knot Challenge!

KNOT MY JOB CHALLENGE:

A gang of outlaw bikers is invading your town. Can you tie a line across the road between two trees or logs in time to trip up the bandits?

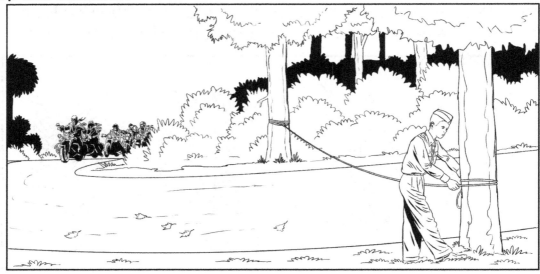

/JTM/MISSIONOPS/KNOTMYJOB

Lay out what you will tie to, a log or branch perhaps the back of your minivan and for the other end you're stretching across the road where the biker gang will approach attaching to another pole, tree or stationary object. Something that has a loop or hook on it and will provide some weight to pull against. Have your C.O. or other officer time your challenge.

CHALLENGE STEPS:

A. Tie a bowline knot at the end of the rope.

B. Untie the bowline knot because you realize you don't need this knot!

C. Tie a buntline hitch around a log

D. Take the rest of the line and you'll tie it to a hook or eye using a butterfly loop and a trucker's hitch and pull tight so that the bikers will fly right over their handlebars.

E. Celebrate the liberation of your town!

HELPFUL KNOT TERMS:

Bight: a U-shaped curve or bend in a rope
Running End: The end of the rope or the free end
Standing Part: The rope other than the Running End
Half Hitch: also known as an overhand knot

MISSION VALUE:

» +250 MAN POINTS FOR TYING EACH TYPE OF KNOT

» +1000 MAN POINTS COMPLETING THE CHALLENGE IN 1 MIN

» +500 MAN POINTS COMPLETING THE CHALLENGE IN 2 MIN

OPERATION AVOCATION
RESEARCH AND DEVELOP A NEW HOBBY

MISSION BRIEF:

After a reconnaissance mission to your local library, your mission is to research, choose and explore a new hobby or pastime.

EQUIPMENT:

A library card (you can get one at the library if you don't already have one), your mission notebook and whatever you might need for your new hobby.

MISSION DETAILS:

Developing a new hobby or interest is a great way to battle boredom. This mission is to develop a new hobby in your life apart from any form of screen such as computers, tablets, cell phones or TV. Doing a little research at the library you'll discover a whole new world of interests and

hobbies then you could imagine.

01. LIBRARY RECONNAISSANCE

Have your C.O. drop you off at checkpoint
Lima AKA the library.

If you don't know where your local library is, do some
research to find out and plan the trip for you and your C.O.
Work out with your Commanding Officer what window of
time you have at the library (2 hours is a good start) and plan
your research accordingly.

02. RESEARCH HOBBIES

Your library will undoubtedly have a computer searching
system to locate books. Do some searches on topics you
are interested in identifying the location of the book in the
library. Alternately you can talk to a librarian who would
be absolutely thrilled to help you locate some resources on
hobbies and might have some excellent insight on sections
of the library you can browse. Look below for a variety of
suggestions to stir your imagination.

03. CHOOSE A HOBBY

In your mission notebook write what you've learned about
your chosen hobby. What equipment would you need if any?
Who could you talk to and learn more about this hobby?
Are there groups of people who might work on this hobby
together?

HOBBY IDEAS

- ❑ Amateur Radio
- ❑ Archery
- ❑ Astronomy
- ❑ Autograph Collecting
- ❑ Beekeeping
- ❑ Bicycling
- ❑ Billiards
- ❑ Bird Watching
- ❑ Boating
- ❑ Boomerang Throwing
- ❑ Bow Making
- ❑ Break Dancing
- ❑ Camping
- ❑ Canoeing
- ❑ Chess
- ❑ Chip Carving
- ❑ Coin Collecting
- ❑ Collecting World Money
- ❑ Comic Books
- ❑ Cooking
- ❑ Dioramas
- ❑ Disc Golf - Disc Throwing
- ❑ Drawing
- ❑ Fencing
- ❑ Film Making
- ❑ Fishing
- ❑ Fishkeeping
- ❑ Fly Fishing
- ❑ Gardening
- ❑ Geocaching
- ❑ Ham Radio
- ❑ Hiking
- ❑ Hunting
- ❑ Ice Skating
- ❑ Insect Collecting
- ❑ Juggling
- ❑ Keychain Collecting
- ❑ Kite Making
- ❑ Knife Making
- ❑ Knife Throwing
- ❑ Knitting
- ❑ Knot Tying
- ❑ Foreign Languages
- ❑ Leather Working
- ❑ Marbles
- ❑ Magic
- ❑ Marksmanship - Shooting
- ❑ Martial Arts
- ❑ Metalworking
- ❑ Metal Detecting
- ❑ Meteorology
- ❑ Model Building
- ❑ Model Railroading
- ❑ Musical Instruments
- ❑ Sports - Traditional and New to You
- ❑ Origami
- ❑ Painting
- ❑ Parkour
- ❑ Pets
- ❑ Photography
- ❑ Poker
- ❑ Pottery
- ❑ Remote Control Cars, Planes, Boats
- ❑ Rock Collecting
- ❑ Rocketry
- ❑ Running
- ❑ Ship in a Bottle Building
- ❑ Sports Card Collection
- ❑ Stamp Collecting
- ❑ Weight Training
- ❑ Wood Burning
- ❑ Wood Carving
- ❑ Wood Working
- ❑ Yo-Yo Skills

04. EXPLORE YOUR HOBBY

Begin a rewarding journey to become an
expert in your chosen hobby. Whether that's
practicing, looking for more items to collect
or just doing it.

MISSION PARAMETERS:

You should choose a hobby that genuinely interests you.
Maybe you need some equipment to go along with your new
interest, Operation Kickstart might help you get some funds.
Hobbies need not be expensive to be enjoyable.

MISSION VALUE:

»   +500 MAN POINTS FOR CHOOSING A HOBBY

»   +500 MAN POINTS FOR DEMONSTRATED STUDY OF YOUR
    HOBBY

OPERATION PERSEVERANCE
DESIGN AND KEEP
A PHYSICAL FITNESS GOAL

MISSION BRIEF:

Your mission is to set a reoccurring exercise goal daily for an entire month. Exercise is a necessary part of anyone's well being and setting goals and achieving them are important lessons for life.

EQUIPMENT:

Whatever you might need to perform your exercise, perhaps a ball, stick and pucks or weights, your mission notebook.

MISSION DETAILS:

Getting started on the mission is simple. Completing the task is another thing entirely.

01. PICK AN ACHIEVABLE FITNESS GOAL

If you play sports, off season training will give you a huge advantage when the season starts. If, for instance, you play hockey taking 100 shots a day will provide you with an edge over teammates who played video games all summer. That would mean you shot over 3000 pucks in 30 days!

Perhaps you play basketball so taking 200 shots a day would be a good goal. Or maybe you see yourself on Ninja Warrior, so 10 pull up's, 30 situp's and 30 pushups a day is your goal. Set a goal and see what you can do every day to beat it.

02. RECORD YOUR PROGRESS

Using your mission notebook, set up a page to record your goal writing the date and how many of what exercise or activity you performed.

MISSION PARAMETERS:

It will be easy not to finish this mission, it takes willpower, focus and determination to complete. It will be so worth it! If you are somewhere where you can't do your full activity, think of a workaround. As an example, if your exercise goal is to shoot baskets but you don't have a hoop handy, do some pushups, situps, run in place, jumping jacks or other exercises. You can do it, cadet!

MISSION VALUE:

» +250 MAN POINTS FOR SETTING YOUR GOAL

» +250 MAN POINTS FOR COMPLETING 7 OF 30 DAYS

» +750 MAN POINTS FOR COMPLETING 14 OF 30 DAYS

» +1500 MAN POINTS FOR COMPLETING 21 OF 30 DAYS

» +3000 MAN POINTS FOR COMPLETING 30 OF 30 DAYS

OPERATION WHEELS ON THE BUS
UTILIZE PUBLIC TRANSPORT
TO REACH A DESTINATION

MISSION BRIEF:

In our original mission Operation Timbuktu, you navigated a mechanized vehicle to a destination. In Operation Wheels On The Bus, you'll use some of your navigation skills to ride public transport to a destination.

EQUIPMENT:

Computer or bus route maps, mission notebook, phone for communication to H.Q.

MISSION DETAILS:

Some Journey to men cadets may be no stranger to public transportation (buses, subways, trains, ferries, etc.) but many more have never ridden their cities transit. You'll start by researching your transit options in your town or nearby city, learn the service area and find a destination

you want to reach and finally take the transport to and from your destination.

01. LEARN HOW TO USE YOUR PUBLIC TRANSPORT

The first step in this mission is to understand what public transit options you have in your city. Your city doesn't have to be large to have some options like bus routes. A quick internet search for "<your city> public transit" should bring up some options. If you have transit in your city what you'll often find is a guide to riding or using those services. For instance, Stanislaus has a helpful guide on using their public bus system that's a great starting point to the new traveler. You'll find out such tips as to where to catch the bus or train, how much it costs and the times it operates.

02. PLAN YOUR TRANSIT ROUTE

This might be the hardest part of your mission depending on how big your transit system is in your area. For instance, in the Seattle region, four different transit authorities work together, but it can be confusing which goes where and how they work together. There is a combination of buses, trains, light rail and ferries that might be required depending on the destination. Fortunately, most of the systems will work together to get you a trip plan.

To begin, you need to know your starting point (typically your address) and then your destination address. Piece of cake. Now you need to find out the nearest route to begin your journey. Most times, you must walk between routes or to the initial nearby stop. Google Maps Transit is an excellent tool for planning routes if there is coverage for your city https://maps.google.com/landing/transit/. It will give you

suggestions on routes and bus numbers and times. Useful stuff although your local transit authority might have a trip planner application or guide available.

At this stage, you'll want to write information about your trip in your mission notebook. If you have a timetable or route from your planning website, you will want to print it off.

03.   PRESENT YOUR TRIP TO YOUR C.O.

To get your travel permit, you need to talk to your C.O. about your trip and demonstrate your knowledge of the public transit process. Give them the details of the route, which transport option you are riding, how much it will cost, where you are going and when you'll be back. Also, talk about your communication strategy and who is going on the trip with you and how you will be safe. We highly recommend the buddy system.

04.   BE SAFE

In most cases, public transportation is safe, but also know your surroundings and take some steps to make sure you are being smart about your trip. Don't talk to strangers. Don't wear headphones or bury your head in your phone, you need to know what's going on around you especially if you are traveling through unfamiliar territory.

If you are carrying money or your wallet, keep it in your front pocket.

If there is any problem at all inform the bus driver or train conductor immediately and they'll help you.

05.   TRAVEL TO YOUR DESTINATION

Now it's time to get traveling. Be sure you have a phone available to communicate to base your whereabouts and provide positional updates.

MISSION PARAMETERS:

If you have public transportation available, it can be a gateway to a whole new world and freedom but only if you are a responsible and smart rider. Showing your knowledge of the public transit system and your overall plan is a critical component of getting trip approval.

MISSION POINTS:

» +1000 MAN POINTS FOR SUCCESSFULLY PLANNING AND PRESENTING YOUR TRIP

THE MACGYVER CHALLENGE
SAVE THE VILLAGE
FROM NOXIOUS GAS ANTS

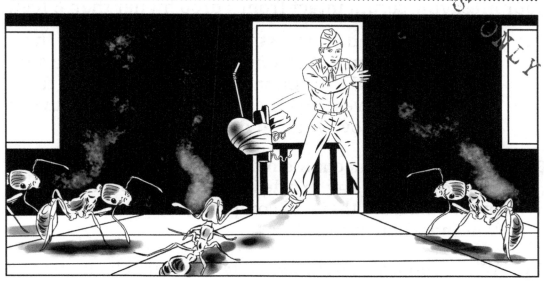

MISSION BRIEF:

An enormous colony of a previously undiscovered Egyptian Gas Ant has infested your village of Journeyton, and you're being called in to save the day. You parachute into the infectious disease lab only to find it's exposed to the deadly gas except for a small room and a deck outside the lab. You must get the serum safely to the National Guard who is waiting below your building but how will you do it with only 60 minutes and the supplies you've found in the closet?

EQUIPMENT:

Swiss Army Knife, eggs and various building materials. This is up to the C.O. to determine the resources available during the mission. Some sample items: Gorilla Tape, tongue depressors, gauze bandages, paracord, bendy straws.

MISSION DETAILS:

Using the materials you have found on-site you have only 60 minutes to build a contraption that can keep the egg holding your lifesaving serum intact from a drop higher than 6 feet.

01.   Get your egg and build a structure around it with the materials on hand. A strong suggestion is to use a soft padded material to cushion your egg. Using duct tape or other adhesives directly on the egg will make it very difficult to remove without destroying it.

02.   Think about a mechanism that will provide a nice soft cushion for the egg to ride in and then provide an outer structure that will compress and absorb the hard landing when dropped.

03.   When you finish building your structure clean up your other materials and return to a sack or garbage bag, you have in your work area.

04.   When time expires work with your C.O. to document your serum drop from 6 feet or higher. If you are standing on a ladder, please be safe. Get photo proof of your serum holder and your drop.

DROP THE SERUM!

You are now clear to exit the lab retrieve your serum and verify it's intact. Be careful when opening your mechanism so you don't accidentally break the egg while removing its outer structure.

MISSION PARAMETERS:

You cannot leave your lab safe area during the 60 minutes.

/JTM/MISSIONOPS/MACGYVER

Communications are offline so your efforts to reach outside help are futile. If your serum egg breaks during the build process, you can use another, but you will lose half of the mission value.

MISSION VALUE:

» +500 MAN POINTS FOR BUILDING THE SERUM HOLDER

» +1500 MAN POINTS FOR YOUR EGG SURVIVING THE 6 FOOT DROP

» +500 MAN POINTS FOR A PARTIALLY INTACT EGG AFTER THE DROP

» -500 MAN POINTS FOR LEAVING A DIRTY WORK AREA INCLUDING EGG RESIDUE

OPERATION FALLING WATER
BUILD A WATER BALLOON LAUNCHER

MISSION BRIEF:

Your mission is to construct a device suitable for launching water balloons over long distances. Directions cover building our model but feel free to improvise and implement your own designs.

EQUIPMENT:

4 feet of surgical tubing or exercise bands or polespear rubber tubing, duct tape (Gorilla tape strongly recommended), towel or tarp or other heavy fabric approximately 15"x15", 5/8" dowel or scrap of wood approximately 18" long, saw, scissors, water balloons, EYE PROTECTION!

MISSION DETAILS:

Any cadet worth their salt is always looking to expand the armory. In this mission, you'll be developing a water balloon launcher. It's not complicated, and you can use household items for construction. Feel free to experiment with different materials and construction techniques. The trickier equipment is the surgical tubing or Polespear tubing. You can find surgical tubing in the fishing section of many megastores or your neighborhood outdoor store. You could use exercise bands as another option. The best choice for long distance launching is polespear rubber tubing which is very difficult to find locally but is incredibly durable and springy.

01. LAYOUT AND CUT THE TOWEL AKA BALLOON HOLDER

Using our towel cutout plan use a pen or marker to make your cutting lines. These are just suggested dimensions but are big enough to hold a standard water balloon.

Cut the four corners out with your scissors. You can also cut the towel to size if necessary.

TOWEL CUT OUT

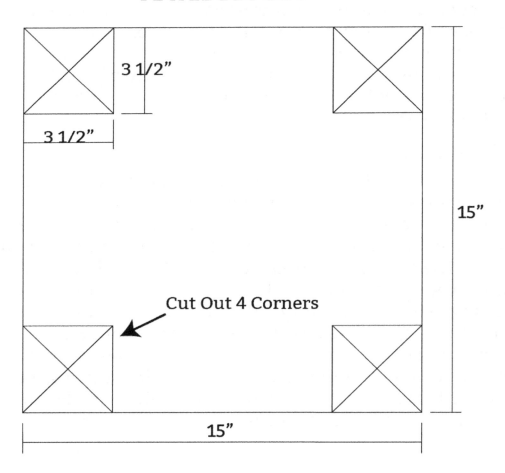

3 1/2"

3 1/2"

15"

Cut Out 4 Corners

15"

02.   PUT YOUR HANDLES IN PLACE

Place the dowels on the two sides of your
tabs and tape into place with your duct tape.
Just know when building the launcher you
can't use too much duct tape. Your water balloon launcher
will be much stronger if you use a generous amount of tape.
At this point just be sure not to tape up the other tabs, those
will be used to run your tubing through in step 3.

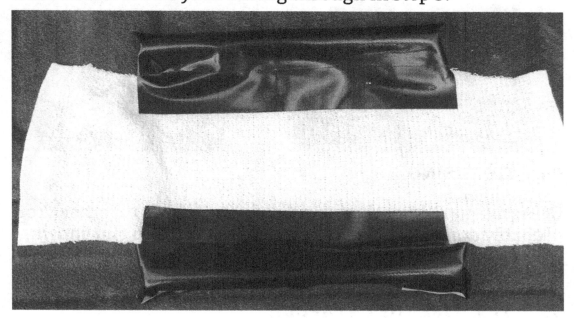

03.   INSTALL TUBING

Now you follow a similar process locking your pipe into place
on your launcher being careful not to tape the tubing to your
launching pouch. The tubing should be able to move freely.
Fold over the towel tab sandwiching the tubing into place
and tape generously. You'll notice in our picture we've left
the center untaped as it provides a softer area to cradle your
water balloons avoiding friendly fire during loading.

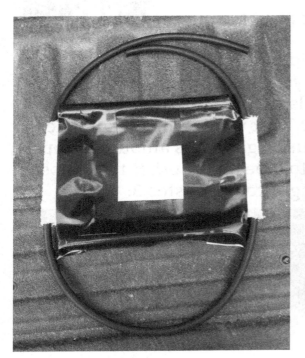

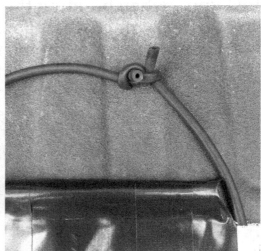

04.   TIE TUBING

Using a square knot tie the ends of your tubing together. You probably don't need the overhand knots on each end shown, but you want to keep a close eye on this knot as you are launching. Getting slapped in the face by your tubing hurts.

05.   TEST FIRE THE CATAPULT!

Put on your safety glasses. You can use the dowels or handles to hold or alternately you can use the tubing side. You'll need two buddies to man each side of the catapult, or a buddy and a tree. When you are preparing to launch, it's best to pull down and back keeping the balloon in place and let it rip! Please be careful of what you are aiming at, these water balloons can seriously hurt humans or pets, so aim near them, not right at them, give them a good splash.

MISSION PARAMETERS:

The tape is the key here, a good quality duct tape will make this work really well. We always recommend Gorilla Tape as it's incredibly strong and durable.

MISSION VALUE:

»   +1000 MAN POINTS FOR MAKING YOUR LAUNCHER

»   -250 MAN POINTS FOR HITTING ANYONE AT CLOSE RANGE

»   -250 MAN POINTS FOR NOT CLEANING UP YOUR WORK AREA OR SPENT WATER BALLOONS

OPERATION CORRESPONDENCE
WRITE A LETTER TO A RELATIVE

MISSION BRIEF:

If you can't be with your beloved Grandmother in person, few things will mean as much to her as a handwritten letter from one of her favorite people in the world, you. In this mission, you'll write a properly formatted letter and send it to someone you love.

EQUIPMENT:

Stationery for the letter, pen, envelope, stamp.

MISSION DETAILS:

We will not get hung up on style guides and the proper formatting of a letter, your Aunt will not care about that anyway, the content is the important bit. We'll tackle the message in parts.

01.   GATHER MATERIALS

A piece of notebook paper just will not cut it, at the very least get a new piece of paper from your printer, even better some beautiful stationery designed just for sending notes and letters. You know something with some adorable cats playing with string or some sad clowns. You also need a pen. No crayons, markers or pencils, you're writing a letter dang it.

02.   DATE

Put the day you're writing the letter up in the left corner like this:

July 24, 2019

03.   THE GREETING OR SALUTATION

This is where you open your letter, Dear Grandpa, or Dear Beloved Aunt, are good examples. Don't use Hello or Hi as your salutation, we're going to up our game a bit here, this isn't an email.

04.   LETTER BODY

Now it's up to you to write something interesting to your loved one. You could start with what's going on in your life. Sports or activities you're doing. Maybe how you're doing with your Journey to Men missions.

You could also thank this relative for the impact they've had on your life. "I just wanted to thank you for always coming to my break dancing recitals. It makes me feel good you care so much about me to be there." Perhaps they got you a cool gift for your birthday or taught you something useful.

Ask them some questions about them based on things you know they like. You might get a letter in return answering your questions.

05.   CLOSING

Examples include: Love, or Sincerely, and then sign your name below that.

06.   ADDRESS AND MAIL ENVELOPE

You put your address on the top left of your envelope and right in the middle your loved one's name and address. Slap an appropriate stamp on there and get it in the mail!

MISSION PARAMETERS:

Don't you dare type this out on the computer! This mission is for a handwritten note. If you mess up and need to cross some things out, you'll be better off just to copy the letter on a new piece of paper. Odds are good your loved one will save this letter, so you want it to look neat. See below for an example letter, don't copy the sample!

MISSION VALUE:

»   +1000 MAN POINTS FOR WRITING A LETTER

»   +250 MAN POINTS FOR EACH ADDITIONAL LETTER WRITTEN

July 24, 2019

Dear Beloved Grandma,

I'm writing some interesting stuff here about what's going on. You'll be so surprised at what happened the other day when my <insert pet here> did <interesting thing>.

Thank you for <something really cool> It helped me to do <something neat>..

Interesting question about Grandma here.

Cool things you appreciate about your Grandma here.

Love,

Paul

OPERATION FOXHOLE
DIG A FIGHTING HOLE TO SURVIVE
A FRONTAL ASSAULT

MISSION BRIEF:

The military has used foxholes in warfare since World War I to protect soldiers from gunfire, artillery, tanks, and other dangers. Your mission is to dig an entrenchment that will allow you to survive a frontal assault by your C.O. or other attackers.

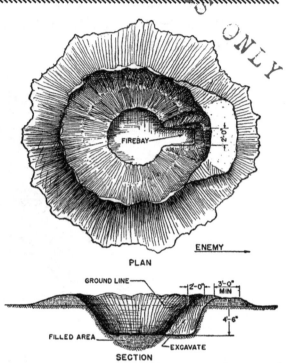

FIGURE 60.—Shell-hole position, showing improvements for one man.

EQUIPMENT:

Entrenching tool or shovel, defensive weaponry (optional), suitable foxhole digging area.

MISSION DETAILS:

01. Review the different entrenchment options in this mission guide. You can build a prone trench, a shell hole position or a stand-up foxhole (1 man or larger). A key component of entrenchment digging is the ability to use it at any time no matter how far into the digging you have progressed. The enemy isn't necessarily going to wait until you've completed digging your hole before they attack.

02.   Find a suitable location for digging
      your hole, that's not too near trees (you
      don't want to dig through roots) that
      has protection from the back and will
      provide decent camouflage. Be sure
      you have your C.O.'s permission to begin your
      excavation.

FIGURE 59.—Prone shelter.

03.   Remove any turf around your defensive position before
      digging the deeper hole. You can ease your shovel
      under the vegetation and set it aside, it will keep the
      foliage alive and will mask your digging efforts at the
      final phase when it's placed on the fresh soil around
      your foxhole.

04.   Trace out your hole on the ground using your shovel.
      Dig placing the dirt removed around the perimeter of
      your marked location. This is going to take significant
      physical effort, but remember your life just might
      depend on it. If you are digging with a buddy, take
      turns digging the hole and spreading the soil around

the perimeter. Perfect camouflage would mean the foxhole is not readily visible to casual observers.

05. Prepare your defenses. It's up to you what armaments to equip your entrenchment, Nerf guns, Airsoft rifles, water balloons. You never know what will come after you.

06. Defend your position! You will come under attack, be sure to use the cover of your fighting hole to avoid injury. Retreat is not an option!

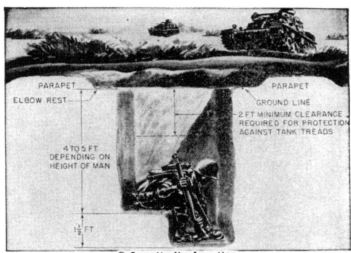

① Longitudinal section.

07. Negotiate with your C.O. on the future of your fighting hole. If they allow you to leave it in place, it would be wise to cover with a piece of plywood or another sturdy roof to keep innocents from falling into the hole. Otherwise, return the hole to its previous non-hole state.

MISSION VALUE:

» +1000 MAN POINTS FOR A WELL DUG HOLE

» +1000 MAN POINTS FOR SURVIVING AN ENEMY FRONTAL ATTACK

» +250 MAN POINTS FOR SUCCESSFULLY RETURNING FIRE

» -250 MAN POINTS FOR LEAVING A MESSY WORK AREA

OPERATION TIME CRISIS
MANAGE YOUR TEAMS TIME SCHEDULE
AND SAVE THE TOWN

MISSION BRIEF:

Bad news cadet, there has been a re-infestation of Egyptian gas ants in your neighboring town. The department of civilian health is trucking in a critical shipment of antidote to your location, but due to the explosive nature of the serum, it has to be received precisely at the stated time to its shipment location. Your assignment is to schedule your local squad's schedule for the day being sure to meet the shipment on time at the specified location.

EQUIPMENT:

Some form of timekeeping device: a wristwatch, an atomic clock, sundial. Mission notebook and a writing instrument.

MISSION DETAILS:

"If you're not 15 minutes early, you're late."
Time management is an important skill to
develop for most anything you will do in
your life. Flying on a plane, working a job, landing on the
moon all require that you arrive on time and often early.
Working with your C.O. you will develop an entire day's
schedule from waking up until you lay your head down in
your bunk at the day's end. You are responsible for yourself
and the rest of your squad arriving and departing on time
from each of your various stops throughout the day.

01.   DAY BEFORE PLAN DAYS SCHEDULE

Time management takes planning plain and simple. Working
with your C.O. you must figure out the next day's activities.
It might help just to make a list of all the things you need to
do to start. Be sure to include: receive gas ant serum as a key
schedule item. Don't worry about the details yet you are just
trying to understand all the working pieces of your squads
calendar.

02.   CREATE MISSION SCHEDULE

Included in your mission packet is a blank time schedule you
can use to plan your day. One challenge of time scheduling
is the behavior of your squad. If your little brother would
rather spend 30 minutes in the bathroom pretending he's
scuba diving, then getting ready for the day you need to
allow proper time for that. You might need to wake him
earlier than usual.

You also must make sure you plan enough time for travel
to and from your activities, this should all be part of your
schedule. Think through all the items on your list and give

yourself some extra time to be sure you hit your timeline.

03.   EXECUTE YOUR SCHEDULE

Your mission day has begun hopefully with you waking up at the right time. It's your duty to manage the squads activities. This does not give you permission to boss everyone around but encourage with great enthusiasm.

As your day progresses check off each task noting whether you were on-time. If you miss one of your times, you can adjust the rest of the schedule to accommodate just inform your C.O. of the change. Keep an eye on your rendezvous with the antidote shipment!

04.   COMPLETE YOUR MISSION

After completing your day's mission, tally up your man points and get to sleep at your assigned time resting peacefully knowing once again you've saved the town from those terrible insects.

MISSION VALUE:

» 500 MAN POINTS FOR CREATING A SCHEDULE

» 200 MAN POINTS FOR EACH SUCCESSFUL TIME EVENT

» 1000 MAN POINTS FOR RECEIVING THE SERUM ON TIME

» -100 MAN POINTS FOR EACH CHECKPOINT MISSED

TIME	TASK	ON-TIME?
7:30 AM	Wake up	Yes
7:40 AM	Watch cartoons with Johnny	Yes
8:15 AM	Have breakfast with squad	No
9:00 AM	Get dressed, brush teeth, feed the dog	Yes
9:30 AM	Drive to Tae Kwon Do practice	Yes
9:45 AM	Tae Kwon Do practice	Yes
11:00 AM	Drive to Burger World for lunch	Yes
11:15 AM	Eat lunch	Yes
12:00 PM	Drive Home	Yes
3:00 PM	Drive to Dad's Break-dancing Practice	Yes
4:30 PM	Drive to Grandma's for visit	No
6:00 PM	Have Dinner with Grandma	Yes
6:45 PM	Receive Antidote shipment	Yes!
7:00 PM	Drive back to HQ	Yes
9:00 PM	Hit the sack	Yes

TIME	TASK	ON-TIME?

OPERATION SAFEHOUSE
BUILD AN EMERGENCY SHELTER

Figure 5-3. Poncho Tent With A-Frame

MISSION BRIEF:

In a survival situation shelter is a critical component that can mean the difference between life or death. Your mission is to build a shelter that is big enough for you to lie down inside comfortably and that will protect you from your local dangers such as wind, rain, animals, and marauders.

EQUIPMENT:

Your pocket knife, paracord, a water bottle.

MISSION DETAILS:

The first order of business for building a shelter is site selection. You need to consider your surroundings to make sure your build location is safe thinking about the following things:

» Will it offer protection from wind?

» Will it provide protection from wild animals?

» Is there a danger from falling branches or rocks?

» Is it safe from water? (not in a dry creek bed, flood plain)

» Are adequate materials around the site to build?

TYPES OF SURVIVAL SHELTERS

Let's talk about the kinds of shelters you can build. Depending on your survival situation and materials available you could construct a poncho tent or teepee, an igloo or many options but for our purposes we'll build what the military calls a field-expedient lean-to. Feel free to build a structure of your own design as long as it helps you complete the mission parameters below. Look through this mission guide for other shelter examples you can model. You might find the debris hut is a useful survival shelter in rainy climates. This mission assumes you are in a wooded area with natural materials on hand to make your shelter.

Figure 5-9. Field-Expedient Lean-to and Fire Reflector

01.   CHOOSE YOUR SHELTER SITE

With your design information written in your notebook lets find a good location for your shelter. If possible give your construction a head start by finding an old stump, upright trees, downed trees to use as a construction base. In a

survival situation you might need to quickly erect your shelter and work on a longer term situation at a later time.

02.   GATHER YOUR BUILDING MATERIALS

You'll want to gather up branches, boughs, leaves and what other natural materials you have around to make your shelter. Branches are a key building component for making the structure of your hut, but things like leaves, grasses, and shrubberies work well as insulation for the roof and floor. Don't forget your paracord to lash branches together to make a more sturdy shelter.

03.   BUILD YOUR SHELTER

You've done your preparation work now you just need to get your survival shelter constructed. Start with the overall framework using branches as the supporting members and then using other items on top to insulate or provide protection. As you are building be sure you are doing some of your own testing to be sure it stands up to a little jostling outside. You don't want the shelter to collapse on you while you are in it.

04.   SURVIVE IN YOUR SHELTER

Next, you have to test out your shelter, and that's the job of your C.O.'s. They'll provide a series of tests to see how you fare. Earn extra points by spending the night in your shelter.

MISSION PARAMETERS:

To earn maximum survival points your shelter must pass four separate tests designed to simulate a survival situation. Your C.O.'s will test in four areas:

A. WIND

A blower or the exhaust end of a shop vac can test how adequate the shelter will be in a wind storm. Perform the blowing from a distance of 15 feet to simulate a decent storm.

B. RAIN

A pitcher of water poured over the shelter will simulate a rainstorm.

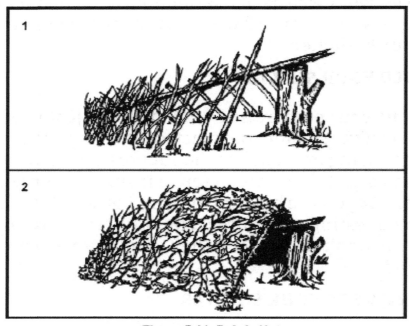

Figure 5-11. Debris Hut

C. FALLING DEBRIS

A regular size branch being thrown onto the shelter is a good test for falling debris.

D. WILD ANIMALS

If you have a dog in the house turn them loose to see if they can enter the shelter, alternately a squadmate can simulate a wild animal trying to enter your shelter.

MISSION POINTS:

» +1000 MAN POINTS FOR BUILDING A SHELTER

» +250 MAN POINTS FOR SURVIVING THE WIND TEST

» +250 MAN POINTS FOR SURVIVING THE RAIN TEST

» +250 MAN POINTS FOR SURVIVING THE BRANCH TEST

» +250 MAN POINTS FOR SURVIVING THE WILD ANIMAL TEST

» +1000 MAN POINTS FOR SPENDING THE NIGHT IN YOUR SHELTER

/JTM/MISSIONOPS/SKIDMARK

put them on hangers or fold if you store them in drawers.

MISSION VALUE:

» +1000 MAN POINTS FOR SUCCESSFULLY WASHING YOUR CLOTHES

» +1000 MAN POINTS FOR SUCCESSFULLY DRYING YOUR CLOTHES

» +500 MAN POINTS FOR PUTTING YOUR CLOTHES AWAY

» -1000 MAN POINTS FOR LEAVING CLOTHES IN DRYER OVERNIGHT

About the Author

Paul Van Lierop is a husband and father of three who resides in the beautiful environs of Montana. He is at heart an outdoorsman, a hobbyist, a technologist and a lover of ice hockey. While his background is not full of collegiate level parenting credentials he has been successfully parenting his kids for eighteen years. He has been a youth hockey coach for over 6 years and previously established the Watch D.O.G.S. program at his local elementary school. Mostly he enjoys spending time with his family.

Made in the USA
Middletown, DE
05 August 2019